D0903113

Leisure & Urbanism
In Nineteenth-Century Nice

Leisure & Urbanism
In Nineteenth-Century Nice

C. James Haug

THE REGENTS PRESS OF KANSAS
LAWRENCE

Publication of this book has been aided by a grant from the
National Endowment for the Humanities

Library of Congress Cataloging in Publication Data

Haug, C. James, 1946—
Leisure & urbanism in nineteenth-century Nice.
Bibliography: p.
Includes index.
1. Tourist trade—France—Nice.
2. Nice (France) —History.
I. Title.
II. Title: Leisure and urbanism in nineteenth-century Nice.
G155.F8H38   381'.459144941   81-15780
ISBN 0-7006-0221-6   AACR2

for
R. J. H.
C. C. H.
and
C. M. H.

Contents

Illustrations

MAPS

COMPUTERGRAPHIC IMAGES

Acknowledgments

THIS BOOK COULD NOT HAVE BEEN WRITTEN without assistance from many people living in both Europe and the United States. Their friendship, counsel, and criticism is much appreciated.

Monographs usually rely heavily on material available only in archives, and this work is no exception. Both Ernest Hildesheimer, the archivist of the Archives départementales des Alpes-Maritimes, and Madame Mireille Massot, the archivist of the city of Nice, made their collections readily available. Madame Hellé Mélandri, assistant archivist of the city of Nice, and the late Mme. Andrée Devun, *Documentaliste-Archiviste* of the Archives départementales des Alpes-Maritimes, were extraordinarily helpful. They helped me gain access to sources that otherwise would have been unavailable and facilitated the process of archival research in many other ways.

I would especially like to thank those fellow historians who have offered advice and criticism while this book has been in progress. The book owes its inception to conversations with Charles K. Warner and Ambrose Saricks. Others have read drafts of the manuscript and have offered useful suggestions. Martin Schaffner of the Historisches Seminar of the University of Basel, Frances Malino of the University of Massachusetts at Boston, Ambrose Saricks of the University of Kansas, and John Marszalek and Edmond Emplaincourt of Mississippi State University read portions of the manuscript and helped me sharpen interpretations and avoid factual mistakes. Thomas Kellog provided much useful advice. The contributions of all these friends and scholars is much appreciated.

This work could not have been completed without the help of several institutions. Research grants from the Graduate School of the University of Kansas and the Office of Research and Graduate Studies and the Institute for the Humanities at Mississippi State University helped at various stages. The University of Kansas provided all requested data processing resources, and Professor R. E. Nunley of the Department of Geography of the University of Kansas put the computergraphic capabilities of the Multi-Dimensional Analysis Processing System at my disposal. Finally, The Travel Research Association, which awarded parts of this work its annual Wesley Ballaine award and permitted me to present some of my conclusions to an audience of travel-industry professionals, must also be thanked.

The final and most important acknowledgment, however, must go to my wife, Ruth, whose unwavering assistance has helped make this whole endeavor possible. Besides assisting with the technical work involved—coding data, typing drafts, and proofreading—she has constantly helped me sharpen ideas that were good and discard those that were bad. Her extensive historical training has made her more of a partner than an assistant, and without her help this study would have been much less.

Introduction

THE PHENOMENON OF TOURISM is one of the most dynamic and powerful creations of Western industrial society. This society's tendency to compartmentalize work and recreation, its ability to move vast numbers of people from place to place with extraordinary speed, and the intense curiosity about far away places generated by mass communications have made recreational travel a commonplace part of everyday life. The annual paid vacation has made a trip to the beach or mountains almost an automatic part of the annual cycle for families of even modest means. Today, recreational travel has become almost a duty, and the economies of countless localities would collapse if it ended.

Indeed, many towns and regions have devoted enormous efforts to making themselves centers for tourism. It is, after all, an immensely appealing industry. Usually, natural attractions form the initial basis for a tourist economy. An area devoid of commerce, industry, and mineral or energy resources can thrive by capitalizing on its natural beauty or climate. Poverty-stricken mountain valleys and fishing villages have been transformed overnight by invading skiers or sun-worshippers. These visitors create jobs, revitalize moribund economies, and contribute greatly —if selectively—to regional prosperity. Isolation and distance from urban centers often are assets to budding resorts, and many obscure parts of the world have found tourism to be the sole remunerative activity open to them. In fact, according to some computations, tourism is now the largest single component in world foreign trade.[1]

In spite of the important role played by tourism, few historians have studied the phenomenon itself or the development of those areas where the industry has had its greatest impact.[2] Put off, perhaps, by the tide of fluffy essays detailing the coming and going of kings, princes, and socialites that flows from the antiquarian press, historians have not often viewed the questions associated with tourism as a fruitful field for investigation. This is unfortunate because considered and realistic evaluations of modern tourism can be made only when the historical development of the industry is known. One reason that modern tourist centers sometimes come to grief seems to be their lack of knowledge about the impact of tourism on other economies, regions, and cities that have become dependent on the industry.

This book is also a contribution to the history of leisure, another neglected area. Recreation absorbs a large part of many modern lives, and people spend much of their leisure time in areas specifically organized and developed for leisure activities. A leisure-oriented locality naturally responds to different imperatives than does, for example, an industrial or administrative center: that very uniqueness requires examination. This book focuses on Nice, the first major city of the modern Western world to become dependent on an economy based on tourism. Here, Nice's goals, aspirations, successes, and failures are examined as it haltingly felt its way along an uncharted path. Nice was the first of its breed; it could not rely on the experience of other cities in making those irrevocable choices that shaped its future.

The kind of tourism that made nineteenth-century Nice a great resort is somewhat difficult for people used to twentieth-century tourism to understand. The French call it *villégiature,* a word that describes the kind of long-term visit enjoyed by most eighteenth- and nineteenth-century visitors to Nice.[3] To live *en villégiature* was a luxury available only to the wealthiest members of society. The day when most people could look forward to an annual vacation had not yet arrived, and Nice's visitors belonged to an elite group whose wealth and income usually did not depend on their personal efforts. For these landowners or investors, a long winter stay in Nice was one of the greatest luxuries available. Nice's winter residents, her *hivernants,* would usually arrive in late October or early November, settle down in their villas or hotels, and remain in the city until the following March or April when they would return to their homes or go to channel or Alpine resorts in northern Europe to spend the summer. They had no interest in the Riviera's summer sunshine, considered Nice's summer climate to be pestilential, and left the city's hotels and beaches deserted.

The *hivernants,* themselves, however, are not the main focus of this work, and the kings, princes, and socialites who visited Nice only occasionally find their way into the narrative. As a rule they did little that was noteworthy. Depending on their preferences, they spent most of the time worrying about their health, taking walks and carriage rides, attending parties and balls, or gambling and carousing. Most of these visitors did not lead particularly interesting or noteworthy lives while residing in Nice, nor is there any reason why they should have. The individual activities that interest posterity usually involve the exercise of political, economic, diplomatic, or intellectual power, or the use of influence that somehow changed the lives of contemporaries or of future generations. Hardly anyone came to Nice to exercise power or to make decisions more important than choosing a dinner menu or deciding which formal gown to wear. Yet collectively, these visitors exercised enormous power over Nice. Their preferences regarding private health, comfort, housing, sustenance, and entertainment forced their host city to respond—and in doing so, to make difficult and expensive choices. Thus, the tourists, while not very interesting individually, are intensely so, taken together. They provided a force that was constantly evolving, changing, and moving—a force that the citizens and officials of Nice learned had the power to create and to destroy.

Nice's attractiveness to its visitors was the product of several factors, but most important among them was the city's mild winter climate. Nice lies on a narrow coastal plain at the foot of the Maritime Alps, which emerge abruptly from the sea and rise to high elevations only a few miles north of the city. These mountains have the dual effect of blocking out the cold winter winds of the north and retaining the warmth released by the Mediterranean. No winter wind comparable to the mistral of the Rhône Valley disturbs the plain of Nice, and the city's winter temperatures, while not warm when compared to modern tropical resorts, are much milder than those in northern Europe. The mean winter temperature in Paris, for example, is 39° F, while the mean winter temperature in Nice is 49° F. It seldom freezes in Nice; fogs are rare; and, although a considerable amount of rain falls during the winter, it usually falls in torrents and runs off quickly.

Nice's most valuable climatic attraction, however, is the extraordinary amount of sunshine that the city enjoys each year. Raoul Blanchard, the foremost geographer of the Alpine region, has calculated that over a ten-year period Nice received more than 2,800 hours of sunshine annually. Paris, during the same period, averaged only 1,000 hours annually. During the autumn and winter these differences are even more pronounced: in December, for example, Paris averaged only 46 hours of sunlight, while Nice averaged 138 hours—exactly three times as much. This sunshine made Nice a center for climatotherapy in the eighteenth and nineteenth centuries, and thousands came to worship the city's winter sun.[4]

These visitors made Nice one of the fastest-growing cities in Europe between 1860 and 1914, and for much of the nineteenth century it enjoyed the highest growth rate of any major French city (see table 1).

TABLE 1

GROWTH RATES IN MAJOR FRENCH CITIES, 1861–1911
(IN THOUSANDS)

City	1861	1881	% Increase 1861–1881	1911	% Increase 1881–1911	% Increase 1861–1911
Paris	1,696	2,269	34	2,888	27	70
Lyons	319	377	18	460	22	44
Marseilles	261	360	38	551	53	111
Toulouse	113	140	24	150	7	33
Bordeaux	163	221	36	262	19	61
Nice	48	66	38	143	117	198

Sources: B. R. Mitchell, *European Historical Statistics, 1750–1970* (New York: Columbia University Press, 1976), pp. 76–78; "Dénombrements des Alpes-Maritimes (compilation made by the Archives Départementales des Alpes-Maritimes).

Nice's tourist industry was highly labor intensive, and thousands of people flocked to Nice because there were jobs to be had in tourist-related industries and trades.

By the middle of the nineteenth century, Nice's visitors collectively held the prosperity of the city in their hands. When the winter residents did not arrive in large enough numbers, stay long enough, or spend enough money the local economy tumbled. When crowds of them arrived early, stayed late, and spent freely, Nice prospered. Their presence shaped the city's population; their needs defined the strength and orientation of the municipal economy; and their housing preferences structured the urban landscape. In short, they provided the nucleus for the city's economic, demographic, social, and spatial development.

Because of their absolute power over the city, nearly every municipal decision focused on the need to please the *hivernants,* and their real or imagined desires were reflected in the decisions of local officials. Nice's municipal administrators, most of whom were lifelong residents of the city who often lived in the ancient city center, away from the tourists, were absolutely convinced that their main official responsibility was to attract more and more visitors to the city. Most members of Nice's municipal council (Conseil Municipal) and most of the city's mayors were convinced that Nice owed its prosperity to what local people liked to call the "swallows of winter"; and most municipal policies were designed to ensure that these "swallows" would return to the city again and again. A local editor aptly expressed this policy in 1882: "We need," he wrote, "visitors, more visitors, and still more visitors."[5] Thus, to study Nice is to study a city whose political and administrative life was shaped by outsiders.

Although their expectations and needs evolved, the *hivernants* seem to have had a clear idea of what a tourist city should be and what it should provide. They expected warm sunshine and balmy breezes, but they also demanded a high level of municipal organization, services of the finest quality, and superior conditions of public health. The first kind of expectations were matters about which a city government could do little: no amount of administrative effort could make the sun shine or call up fresh sea breezes. Municipal officials could, however, control the quality and quantity of city services and the effectiveness of water mains and sewage drains. Knowing that a comfortable urban environment was important to the *hivernants,* these officials spent large amounts of energy and money trying to meet the visitors' demands.

Thus, the problems faced by a tourist town are different from those encountered in an industrial or maritime city. First, the domination of policy-making by outsiders tended to give a sense of artificiality to urban decision-making. Second, the conflicts that emerged when a wealthy, cosmopolitan population drawn from the leisure class came into contact with the conservative, permanent residents, who had little interest in change, often made adversary proceedings of municipal decisions, pitting those who favored change against supporters of tradition. Third, the evolution and maturation of Nice's tourist population required a well-developed ability on the part of municipal officials to adapt to changing outsiders' perceptions of their city. Finally, Nice's tendency to become a hothouse of development created a boom-and-bust mentality conducive to wide-spread speculation, financial over-extension, and a remarkable propensity toward private and public bankruptcy. Taken together these problems created an atmosphere unique to a tourist town.

Yet from another perspective, the problems that emerged in nineteenth-century Nice were not unique to it or to its tourist-based economy. Other European cities faced problems associated with speculative development, changing attitudes toward public health, and demands for expensive public services. In Nice, however, the problems were more forcibly presented. The rich, well-instructed, and demanding visitors whose needs shaped the city engendered lively public debates and, demanding action, made procrastination difficult. Decisions that could be avoided in other cities had to be taken in Nice. Because of this hothouse atmosphere, Nice provides an ideal arena for studying nineteenth-century urbanism.

1

Tourism and Urbanism in Nice, 1750–1860

IN 1750 WHEN GASPARD JOANINI assumed his duties in Nice as chief administrator from the Italian state of Piedmont-Sardinia, the sleepy town differed little from its neighbors. Nondescript stucco buildings baked by the Mediterranean sun dominated narrow and dingy streets. In some ways Nice was a captive of its physical surroundings. The city was huddled against the west side of the mountain that had supported a castle until Louis XIV's armies razed it during the War of the Spanish Succession. Prevented by the sea from growing to the south, Nice's only open view was to the north and west. In this direction, however, lay the Paillon River, a tiny stream that meandered through a huge gravel bed. Only during heavy storms did the Paillon fill, and then it became a raging torrent. This curious and changeable stream impressed visitors who were used to more stable northern European rivers. Louis XIV's military engineer, Vauban, for example, devoted some thought to the stream during a seige of Nice in 1693: Nice was unfortunate, he concluded, because it was plagued with this miserable stream that did much damage, provided few advantages, and was of little use for either irrigating crops or operating mills.[1]

Nice's eighteenth-century economy reflected the organization of a typical Mediterranean town. In 1754, of the 16,000 people living in Nice, Joanini could find only 25 lawyers, 9 physicians, 9 apothecaries, and 15 wholesale merchants. The only notable industries there made sail cloth, soap, candles, leather goods, and liquor. Besides these few primitive occupations, the population was almost entirely engaged in processing or selling the agricultural produce of Nice's hinterland: grain, wine, olive oil, fruit, and some silk cocoons. The production of these commodities, however, did not meet the needs of the city, and Nice regularly imported grain and wine from upper Piedmont and from France. The region's only exports were olive oil, cocoons, linen, and

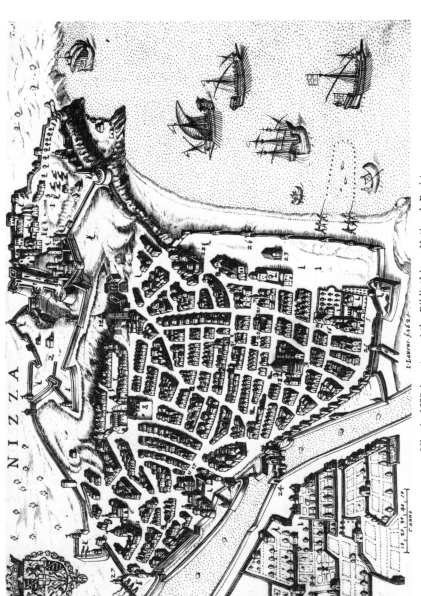

Nice in 1625 *(courtesy of the Bibliothèque National, Paris)*

hemp.[2] Indeed, Nice's commerce was similar to that of neighboring towns which are now little known. Draguignan, for example, had exactly the same distribution of enterprises except for the addition of a small wool industry. And the mountain village of Grasse contained more tanning, weaving, and soap-making businesses than did Nice.[3]

There were several reasons why Nice's economy stagnated during the eighteenth century, but two geographical factors stand out: its unproductive hinterland and its isolation from Europe's urban centers. Nice is located on a narrow coastal plain from which the Maritime Alps rise to form peaks only a few miles inland from the city. These mountains have long been the home of an agricultural population distinguished largely by its poverty. Although fertile valleys are not uncommon in this region, most farmers spent their lives working on terraces that they and their ancestors had hewed from the mountainsides. Most of the region's production went toward feeding its people who, in turn, strove to build more terraces that would support more people. As Fernand Braudel noted, "Life there is possible, but not easy."[4] No matter how hard the people worked, the hinterland of Nice has never been generous, and production has never been sufficient to feed a population of any size.

The coastal plain of Nice, on the other hand, is relatively fertile, and there farmers could produce such traditional Mediterranean crops as oranges, lemons, olives, and silk worms. In the late 1780s, Arthur Young, an Englishman studying French agriculture, found oranges, rosemary, and lavender to be in good supply, but he was shocked at the absence of dairy produce. He described the coastal plain near Cannes, a few miles west of Nice, as a place blessed with a "delicious climate . . . that gives myrtles, oranges, lemons, pomegranates, jassmins, and aloes in the hedges; yet are such countries, if irrigation be wanted, the veriest deserts in the world!" The dry Mediterranean summer made the production of grass and cereals very difficult. "Give me that which will feed a cow," said Young, always the good Englishman, "and let oranges remain in Provence."[5]

The second problem arising from Nice's geography was the difficulty involved in transporting goods to and from the city. Nice did not have easy access to any large population center. The shortest way to Turin, the administrative and political capital of Piedmont-Sardinia, was a winding route over the Maritime Alps. Even in an automobile these mountains are a formidable obstacle, and anyone making the trip can easily see why only intrepid travelers attempted it in the eighteenth century. Arthur Young, who was as intrepid as any, spent four days in a three-passenger carriage on his way from Nice to Turin. He traveled on a new road that had been built in the eighteenth century; the old one was fit only for mules. Despite the new road, however, carriages still could not make the crossing in winter, and mule carts could do so only with extreme caution. This difficulty in communication between Nice and Turin contributed to Nice's isolation. Although Nice was Piedmont's only outlet to the sea and although most of the goods that Turin imported by sea passed through Nice, the fact that all these goods had to be delivered from Nice by mules made it certain that the city would never become a major maritime center. In 1815 when Piedmont-Sardinia received the much more desirable port of Genoa at the Congress of Vienna, it abandoned the port of Nice with considerable relief.[6]

Travel in the Maritime Alps, c. 1820 (*courtesy of the Bibliothèque National, Paris*)

The truth was that in 1750 Nice was just another dusty, provincial Mediterranean town with a mediocre agricultural base, a stagnant economy, and a limited trading future. The beautiful countryside, full of flowers and fruits, and a mild winter climate constituted Nice's only natural resources; and at mid century neither seemed to be of much economic value. Yet, although the residents of Nice took its lovely and temperate surroundings for granted, non-Mediterranean Europeans were impressed, and by the time Young visited Nice in 1789, a small trickle of northern Europeans had already begun arriving there. Attracted by the very resources that the Niçois took for granted, these foreign visitors were willing to pay for the privilege of enjoying Nice's wintertime beauty. Once this connection was properly understood, Nice's fortune was assured.

The first foreigners to realize that the city was an exceedingly pleasant place to pass the winter were those hardy travelers, the English. Nice was, of course, isolated during the eighteenth century, not "on the way" to anywhere. Furthermore, a journey to a far-away place for pleasure or relaxation, while a familiar practice today, was a novel idea in the eighteenth century. Travel was difficult and expensive, and accommodations—other than inns where voyagers could spend an uncomfortable night in the company of the rough characters who frequented the highways—were scarce. Students sometimes took the "grand tour" to finish their educations, and pilgrims visited favorite shrines; but these were excursions with a purpose, and those who undertook them usually did not linger for long after the antiquities had been viewed or the prayers said. Those taking the grand tour had no reason to visit Nice, and few commercial travelers found a trip to the city to be worth the effort. Thus, word of Nice's fine winter climate spread slowly. The Englishmen usually credited with "discovering" Nice were Lord and Lady Cavendish, who visited the city in 1731. (Lady Cavendish was in an advanced state of pregnancy when she arrived in Nice, and while she was there gave birth to a son, Henry Cavendish, who later become famous for his pioneering work in chemistry.) But others believe that the credit should be given to the English officers who passed through Nice in 1746 during the War of the Austrian Succession. They so appreciated the climate that they returned as true *hivernants* after the end of the war. The impact of these early visitors, however, was negligible. They undoubtedly told their friends and associates about their experiences, but knowledge of Nice and its climate was necessarily limited to a small group of wealthy aristocrats, the "jet set" of eighteenth-century society.[7]

The city needed a popularizer, and it found its man in the person of Tobias Smollett, a well-known and prolific writer who by the time of his visit in 1764 had published two popular novels, *The Adventures of Roderick Random* (1748) and *The Adventures of Peregrine Pickle* (1751). He possessed a vigorous and forthright writing style and an observant nature. While wintering in Nice, Smollett began work on a book describing his experiences in southern Europe. *Travels through France and Italy*, which was published in 1766, sold well in England and introduced Nice and its attractions to thousands of Englishmen, who soon began spending their winters there in ever-increasing numbers. Smollett had come to Nice hoping to cure his advanced case of consumption. The air in Nice, he wrote, being "pure, dry, heavy, and elastic must be agreeable to the constitution of those who labour under disorders arising from weak nerves, obstructed perspiration, relaxed fibers, a viscidity of lymph, and a languid circulation." Although Smollett did not find the instant cure he was searching for—and even found himself "visibly wasting" shortly after his arrival—his health soon improved, and he wrote that he could breathe more freely than he had for years.[8]

Smollett's entertaining descriptions of his experiences encouraged many other invalids to seek cures for consumption or other debilitating diseases in Nice, and climatotherapy soon became an important industry. Voltaire, for example, had been advised to go to Nice to reestablish his health, but while praising the air of Nice, he was unwilling to trade the comforts of Ferney for the rigors of an Alpine crossing; and probably realizing that no climate could do much for someone eighty-three years old, he declined to go. Another Frenchman, A.-L. Thomas, a member of the Académie Française and a confidant of Madame Necker, did decide to go and found his visit so beneficial that he made Nice as famous in France as Smollett had in England. Thomas first visited Nice in 1782 and, like Smollett, found the climate invigorating, but hardly capable of working miracles. His first visit did little good. After six weeks, his health had actually worsened to such an extent that he considered leaving. The sea air and the strong, dry winds disagreed with him, and he almost became convinced that those who spoke of Nice as a center for climatotherapy were totally wrong. Thomas persevered, however, and by 1784, wrote that Nice had the most healthful climate in Europe and advised his correspondent, Madame Necker, to try it.[9]

These enthusiastic reports, plus the beneficial effects that visitors had experienced, predictably resulted in the curative powers of Nice's climate being greatly exaggerated. François Emmanuel Fodéré, author of the best eighteenth-century guide to the city, even felt obliged to warn his readers not to harbor unrealistic expectations. No consumptive, he noted, should come to Nice assuming that he would leave in good health. In particular, Fodéré thought that the English seemed to have the greatest confidence in the Riviera's climate. One pathetic example was Joseph Price, an Anglican clergyman who found himself spitting blood after the slightest exertion and who dreamed of a winter in Nice as his last, best hope. In 1792 Price begged the Archbishop of Canterbury to give him an undemanding parish so that he could travel to Nice in search of a miracle.[10]

Indeed, one can only sympathize with the good Vicar Price and other eighteenth-century consumptives who longed for a cure through climatotherapy. Tuberculosis was so pervasive in the urban areas of Europe, so poorly understood, and so incurable through the practice of medicine, that for those who could afford and endure the voyage, a visit to Nice offered the only hope.[11] In retrospect, the argument that raged in both medical and lay circles over the usefulness of climato-therapy was irrelevant. All could see that medical treatment did little for most consumptives, while many who searched for health in Nice found it. Although eighteenth- and early nineteenth-century attempts to turn climatotherapy into a science (so many minutes of sun on the chest, so many deep breaths at 8:00 A.M., etc.) seem absurd, its proponents were right in assuming that rest, clean air, and relief from occupational obligations could only be beneficial. Away from cities, fogs, smoke, and excitement, people like Smollett and Thomas could rest and walk in the sun, far from the cares of London and Paris. Often these exercises brought relief. Many travelers, however, found their illnesses too far advanced to cure; and one of the first duties facing the small English colony in Nice was to build a cemetery. As Emmanuel Fodéré pointed out, it was proof that experiments in climatotherapy too often failed.[12]

Despite Nice's reputation as a center for climatotherapy, the actual number of visitors was small; on the eve of the French Revolution the winter colony included only 115 families. Although the number is not impressive by modern standards, all of these families were wealthy, and many were members of the English or European aristocracy. Usually, these families included numerous children and servants. Some families even brought their private physicians. The impact of these wealthy travelers on Nice was considerable. They expected quality lodging, food, and services for which they were willing to pay well; and the marketplace responded. By the eve of the French Revolution, Arthur Young could find rooms in a local hotel that he was willing to describe as "exceedingly good"—a rare compliment coming from a comfort-loving Englishman who viewed most foreign accommodations with a jaundiced eye.[13]

Throughout the eighteenth century, Nice's foreign colony remained small, in part because of the tedious voyage required to visit the place. Depending on the time of year and the services available, a traveler typically required between one and two weeks to cover the more than 900 kilometers between Paris and Nice. This timetable changed only with the building of railroads. When Smollett visited Nice it took him seven and one-half days to travel from Calais to Lyons, three days to get from Lyons to Avignon, and four days to go from Avignon to Nice. When Charles de Brosses, president of the *parlement* of Dijon, visited Nice in 1739, he spent four days bouncing over the rough terrain between Marseilles and Nice in a series of uncomfortable coaches pulled by starving horses. Although contemporary maps and charts described this as a major post road with eleven relays, in practice it was used mostly by local traffic. "Will it be believed," Young asked rhetorically on the eve of the Revolution, "that from Marseilles with 100,000 souls and Toulon with 30,000, lying in the great road to Antibes, Nice, and Italy, there is no stagecoach or regular carriage?" Unable to find a regular coach, Young booked passage on a boat going from Toulon to Cavalaire, a small town about one-quarter of the way between Toulon and Nice. There Young found neither a coach nor mules or horses to rent; he finally walked to the tiny fishing village of St. Tropez. From there, he got to Nice with the help of several mules, donkeys, and horses. Young, of course, differed from most travelers: he had begun his trip to observe agricultural practices in France, and he was prepared to take his time along the way. Nevertheless, Young's difficulties differed only in degree from those of a winter visitor on his way to Nice.[14]

The trip was also expensive. One historian of French travel has recently computed relative travel expenses in southern France by dividing the cost by the prevailing average hourly wage. According to this study a trip from Paris to Toulouse by stagecoach in 1785 required 1360 hours of labor; for the voyage from Paris to Nice, 1780 hours of labor would have been needed to pay for the eighty relays involved. The stress and tedium of such a trip, combined with its expense, meant that only voyagers well endowed with enthusiasm and money could consider it.[15]

The final obstacle facing an eighteenth-century visitor was the Var River which formed the boundary between France and Piedmont-Sardinia. There was no bridge, and travelers found themselves at the mercy of the residents of Saint-Laurent, a small village on the French side. In 1757, the villagers, who were required by law to transport travelers from one side of the river to the other, turned their responsibility over to a concessionaire who abandoned the traditional boat and instead employed men to carry travelers and their baggage across the river. Each traveler sat on the shoulders of two men who joined arms and waded across. This remained the system for crossing the Var until the French built a shaky bridge after they annexed Nice in 1793.[16]

The nuisances and discomforts associated with overland travel led many of Nice's eighteenth-century visitors to complete the last stage of their voyage by sea. Although usually more comfortable, sea voyages did not lack danger or difficulty. The small coastal craft available at Toulon or Antibes boasted little in the way of amenities and were ill-equipped to deal with storms and rough water. In addition, there were the Barbary pirates. The voyager unfortunate enough to encounter one of these sea-going brigands usually lost his belongings and sometimes was even held for ransom. Despite these dangers, a sea voyage became the more popular method of getting to Nice for those neither afraid of seasickness nor interested in the striking scenery between Marseilles and Nice.[17]

As the popularity of southern France increased in the early nineteenth century, other more accessible towns prospered at Nice's expense. For example, Hyères, a small provincial town near Toulon, achieved some small reputation as a resort for those not courageous or healthy enough to venture the voyage to Nice. Visitors could reach Hyères with relative ease, simply by ferrying down the Rhône. The climate of Hyères was reputed to be beneficial for those suffering from chest diseases in spite of its exposure to the ferocious winter mistral of the Rhône Valley. By mid century a third Riviera town, Cannes, began receiving wealthy travelers fleeing the cold of the North. Cannes is now a world-famous resort, but until 1834 it was a miserable fishing village of some three thousand people, surrounded by dunes and salt pines. Henry Brougham, the Lord Chancellor of England, "discovered" Cannes in 1834 while on his way to Nice. Because cholera was raging in southern France, the Piedmontese police had closed the border. Disappointed, Brougham decided to spend a few days in Cannes. He fell in love with the village, built a luxurious villa, and for the rest of his life was Cannes' most enthusiastic propagandist. Its aristocratic clientele, its peaceful setting, and the fact that the town was in France and not Piedmont, ensured its prosperity.[18]

Neither Brougham nor fellow Britishers had any interest in the village of Cannes itself; similarly, Nice's visitors remained aloof from the city. The English, in particular, showed little interest in integrating themselves into Niçois society, and most *hivernants* avoided the older quarters of the city. The first arrivals found Nice—enclosed by the château on the east and the Paillon on the west—divided into two sections. Visitors found the older section (in effect, the medieval city) intolerable and gravitated toward the newer areas where the streets were wider and the buildings cleaner. At first travelers rented apartments on the streets that ran parallel to the coast. As the city grew toward the mouth of the Paillon, visitors congregated in the newer buildings there, where they found more sun, air, and space than could be had in the older part of the city.[19]

Many of Nice's eighteenth-century visitors wrote travel diaries, and few of them could resist including unflattering descriptions of the Old City: the words *dark, dingy, filthy,* and *squalid* regularly emerge from these travelogues. After France annexed Nice during the Revolution, the government renamed all the streets in an attempt to instill revolutionary zeal in Nice's skeptical population. The dirtiest street of all, occupied by the most miserable people in the city, was named *rue de Bonheur* (Street of Happiness). The revolutionary government gave the rest of the Old City's dirty, lightless, and stinking streets such illustrative names as *rue de la Lumière, rue de Bon Air, rue de la Propreté,* and *rue de la Salubrité*—ironic references to the particular street's reputed light, fresh air, cleanliness, and healthfulness.[20] Needless to say, northern visitors found the buildings bordering these streets unfit for human habitation. A. L. Millin who visited Nice in 1815 (shortly after the Sardinian restoration) pungently described an inspection tour of the Old City where he was greatly impressed with the filthy and nauseating condition of the houses: flies abounded, and the windows of the houses were usually opaque with dirt and flyspecks. Residents who wanted clean windows either had to wash them every day or cover them with silk.[21]

The English *hivernants* kept to themselves as much as possible, avoiding both local people and the non-English members of the tourist colony. Although many of the English visitors were too ill to enjoy a social life of any kind, their haughty aloofness exasperated fellow visitors. "Whether [due to] suspicion or national pride, all familiarity stops in their individual and social relations," wrote one observer in 1843.

> They live absolutely as if they were at Brigton [sic]. During the day they go out—on foot, on horseback, in carriages. Evenings they meet together . . . talk politics, drink tea or drink toasts, but everything in their own way and nearly always without mingling with people of other nationalities.[22]

The English particularly irritated the French. The Abbé Expilly, for example, an influential historian and author, complained that the English made his stay at Nice almost unbearable. Expilly had come to Nice in 1780 to improve his health and found the climate beneficial. The following winter, however, he decided to go to Genoa instead because he had learned that Nice's English contingent would be even larger that year. Moreover, Expilly's pension had been reduced, and he felt that he would not be able to live in a manner sufficient to impress the English who, he thought, evaluated others only in terms of their wealth. "I do not wish," he wrote, "[to give them] a pretext of any kind that will allow them to dare to try to humiliate me." French visitors were irritated nearly as much by the extravagance of the English as by their arrogance. A.-L. Thomas, in a letter to Madame Necker, complained that houses for foreigners were not plentiful because the English would rent them at prices hard to match "when one does not have their guineas."[23]

Although many eighteenth-century visitors preferred to live between the Old City and the Paillon, most chose to live entirely apart from the Old City; by the eve of the French Revolution a tourist colony had begun to spring up to the west, on the Paillon's right bank. Its founders were primarily members of the English colony. Most of their villas were constructed along the route de France, the road leading from Nice to the Var and on to points west. The local name for the region was "Croix-de-Marbre" (a reference to the monument erected there in 1568 commemorating a papal visit). Soon residents spoke of the Croix-de-Marbre area as either "faubourg des Anglais" or "Newborough," depending on whether one spoke French or English. By the Revolution, builders had peppered this quarter with pleasant villas that were close to the sea and surrounded by gardens full of orange, lemon, and fig trees. In 1780 the first English cemetery was located there, just off the route de France.[24]

The peaceful and quiet existence enjoyed by the English winterers ended with the beginning of the French Revolution. After the fall of the Bastille, Nice's English visitors fled; they were soon replaced by another group of travelers fleeing a cold political climate instead of an English winter. These were the émigrés, French aristocrats unable or unwilling to cooperate with the revolutionary government and in need of a haven where they could regroup, consider their resources, and work for the destruction of the Republic. Coblenz was the most famous destination of the émigrés, Nice was another; and by April 1792 around 1,500 émigrés had crossed the Var. The Sardinian government allowed them to use Nice as a staging area and that was enough to convince the revolutionary government that their presence constituted a danger to the Republic. On 28 September 1792, the French armies crossed the Var, the émigrés and the Piedmontese authorities fled, and on 29 September the French entered the city. Nice remained under French control for twenty-two years until the city was returned to Piedmont under terms of the Treaty of Paris in 1814.[25]

The French occupation and the seemingly endless wars undertaken by the republican and imperial governments were disastrous for Nice. These wars curtailed travel within France and ensured that few foreigners, and particularly few British travelers, would be able to visit the city. If the risks of war were not enough to frighten away British visitors, the newly developed hatred of anything British, encouraged by revolutionary zealots, was more than sufficient. In 1794, for example, the revolutionary leaders of Nice, in an apparent effort to eradicate all traces of the British, decided to destroy the small English cemetery. They auctioned all the grave markings to a stonemason who worked them into his buildings. (As a requirement of the sale, the stonemason had to promise to eradicate all signs, letters, or emblems remaining on the grave markers.)[26]

Although the disappearance of most tourists caused considerable hardship for the city, other revolutionary disruptions led to the general impoverishment of the newly established department of Alpes-Maritimes. Conscription of farmers caused food production to drop; maritime blockades curtailed commerce; and France forced the new department, which then included Monaco, to pay heavy taxes to finance both the war and new, French-style institutions. One such institution was the departmental *dépôt de mendicité,* a home for beggars. It was established by order of the imperial government, but financed locally. The home was located in the prince's palace in Monaco, and it drained the resources of the new department. "After having used up all the resources of the communes," wrote the department's advisory council,

> there still remains a deficit of 24,000 that the department must make up each year . . . and by a terrifying debt which aggravates more and more the sad position of its inhabitants, the department will be reduced to the most miserable position possible if we remain required to increase these expenses and sacrifices.[27]

The Peace of Amiens in 1802 provided a brief respite from these depressed conditions, and a handful of English visitors came to spend the winter. Since French suspicion of Britain's peaceful intentions conflicted with Nice's desire for more visitors, the municipal and national governments found themselves at cross-purposes. The prefect of Alpes-Maritimes, Châteauneuf-Randon, tried to make Nice's guests as comfortable as possible while at the same time keeping them under surveillance. As the prefect told the minister of the interior, under the Sardinian regime, the English had been masters of Nice and it would be a difficult task to teach them to leave their spirit of domination behind when they set foot on the soil of the Republic. Unfortunately, neither the French nor the British governments shared Châteauneuf-Randon's conciliatory spirit, and after the breakdown of the Peace of Amiens, the English left. On 22 May 1803 an imperial edict ordered that all Englishmen in France between the ages of eighteen and sixty be arrested as prisoners of war, thus effectively ending tourism until the cessation of hostilities. In spite of French efforts to impress the Niçois with the glories of French citizenship, there is little doubt that most Niçois felt relieved by the fall of the Napoleonic Empire and the end of French domination. The people of Nice, tired of the endless French requisitions for men and supplies and impoverished by the destruction of the tourist trade, hailed the return of Piedmontese administration in 1814.[28]

Two lessons, however, emerged from the revolutionary experience. First, it was clear how much the city had come to depend on tourism and the wealth that the winter visitors brought with them: in twentieth-century economic language, tourism had a multiplier effect on the city's economy. Although relatively small in number, tourists had an impact on Nice's commerce, construction, and services far out of proportion to their numbers. Local officials seemed to realize that visitors were essential if the city were to prosper, that Nice's economic well-being depended on its ability to attract and retain *hivernants*. Second, the Niçois learned that power politics and tourism made unhappy bedfellows. The revolutionary experience clearly demonstrated that a city dependent on foreign visitors had to avoid actions that could jeopardize tourism. Urban self-interest required Nice to exert every effort to direct the national government along conciliatory paths. In part, this helps explain Nice's political conservatism throughout the nineteenth century.

During the years following the Napoleonic Wars, both the permanent and the floating populations of Nice grew rapidly, with most of the growth concentrated on the right bank of the Paillon. The Sardinian government, convinced that without governmental control, urban growth would be disorganized and haphazard, decreed in 1832 that all future construction had to be approved by a new planning commission, the Consiglio d'Ornato, whose members were chosen from among Nice's most prominent citizens. According to its charge, the Consiglio was obligated to "oversee the alignment and the improvement of streets, places, walks, and public monuments; approve plans for new buildings to be erected or buildings to be rebuilt . . . whether in the interior of the city or in the suburbs." But the duties of the Consiglio d'Ornato went far beyond that of a modern zoning commission. All new construction as well as changes in the appearance of existing structures needed the Consiglio's approval. Its chief duty, however, was controlling the growth of Nice's rapidly forming suburbs on the right bank of the Paillon. For this, the Consiglio devised a master plan specifying the direction and width of streets, the height and appearance of buildings, and the placement of public squares. According to historians, no one in Nice could create a public place; develop a street; construct or repair a building; add a door or a window; build a terrace, balcony, or store-front; or erect a sign without permission of the Consiglio.

The Consiglio clearly viewed the whole coastal plain on the right bank of the Paillon as ground for future expansion, an idea which seemed absurd to many Niçois. It further assumed that the area would eventually be completely urbanized thus forming, in effect, a "new city." Accordingly, the Consiglio began laying out streets, beginning with the Paillon and extending toward the Croix-de-Marbre. Infatuated with regularity, the Consiglio insisted that all streets follow a gridiron pattern (just as they did in the typical American city of the period). The Consiglio d'Ornato also had firm ideas concerning urban beauty, which its members apparently derived from inspections of Europe's great cities, and it insisted that Nice's architects and builders pattern their work after models that had succeeded elsewhere. Paris, especially, impressed them, and the Consiglio decided to create a miniature replica of the rue de Rivoli, beginning with the Place Masséna, the new city's hub. All build-ings on this street were required to be of a uniform height and to have porticoes extending over the sidewalk. This imitative attempt failed, and Nice gained only a sun-baked square surrounded by stucco arcades that were more pompous than pleasing.[29]

Nevertheless, the Consiglio had an extremely important effect on the shape of the city. Its unlimited confidence in Nice's future and its belief in the inevitability of rapid expansion meant that it was perfectly willing to lay out streets on land where there were only orange groves and olive trees. This boldness astonished local people who refused to believe that Nice could ever grow very far away from the Paillon. Speculators and builders, who disliked the red tape involved in planned building, opposed the Consiglio's work. Nevertheless, it persevered, enforced its plans, and, as the city grew, enlarged the area included in the master plan. Nice's planned and regulated growth during this period contrasted sharply with other nineteenth-century European and American cities, where speculators and builders determined the pattern of urban growth.[30]

While the Consiglio d'Ornato was trying to make Nice more attrac-tive and appealing to the winter colony, other Sardinian actions seemed calculated to keep visitors away from the city, illustrating the kinds of difficulties that could emerge when traditional local values came in conflict with those of the tourists. An example grew out of a request to construct an Anglican church in Nice. Residents of the English colony, naturally, wished to practice their own religion while living in Nice. Indeed, Protestant ministers regularly accompanied English *hivernants* to Nice. The presence of these Anglican, Methodist, and Presbyterian ministers caused serious concern among Sardinian authorities who felt that their presence might undermine the faith of Nice's good Catholics. The Vatican's chargé d'affaires at Turin sent regular reports to the Pope concerning the religious activities of Nice's English residents; reportedly his observations "gave birth to great worries in the Vatican."[31] Turin refused to allow the English to build a church until 1821, and then only under severe restrictions. The English had to promise to construct their church in a secluded area far from the center of Nice; the church had to have low visibility and could include neither a bell nor a belfry; and its cemetery had to be well hidden by trees and bushes. Only British citizens could enter the church, and all services had to be conducted in English. Quite clearly, the Piedmontese authorities wanted to be certain that the Anglican Church could never rival the established Catholic Church in the eyes of the local people.[32]

The years following the Sardinian restoration were prosperous ones for Nice, a period of gradual and sustained growth. More than ever, Nice's prosperity came from its winter visitors who arrived in ever-increasing numbers. Wealthy, sophisticated, and free-spending, these visitors provided more Niçois with more wealth than workshops and processing facilities had ever produced. Nearly everyone prospered. Builders, construction workers, restauranteurs, and farmers, as well as the owners of hotels, villas, apartments, and land, were able to tap the flow of tourist gold. Even local beggars shared in the new wealth. In 1822, the orange crop failed, and many local laborers who had planned to support themselves by picking oranges turned to begging instead. The English colony was appalled and decided to rid itself of these mendicants by employing them in some useful occupation. The English enjoyed congregating along the seashore between the Croix-de-Marbre and the Old City, so they decided to have the local beggars build a promenade along the sea. These humble efforts temporarily thinned the beggar population and resulted in the beginning of the famous promenade des Anglais, now one of the world's most beautiful drives.[33]

During the first half of the nineteenth century, tourism became increasingly important to Nice because the city's importance to the Sardinian state was decreasing. As part of the 1815 settlement at the Congress of Vienna, Piedmont-Sardinia had received the port of Genoa; Nice's commercial fortunes immediately began to decline. Genoa had a better harbor, a larger and more varied commercial establishment, and better overland links with Turin. Piedmont encouraged importers to channel their goods through Genoa; and as the fortunes of Genoa rose, those of Nice declined. Gradually Nice lost the privileges and immuni-

The Promenade des Anglais, c. 1880 (*courtesy of the Bibliothèque National, Paris*)

ties it had enjoyed while serving as Piedmont's chief port. In 1822 it lost its right to import wheat without paying customs duties; and in 1851, as part of an effort to standardize fiscal procedures throughout the Sardinian states, Nice lost its status as a free port, the last remnant of its ancient independence. Nice, moaned merchants and farmers, was destined to "become the Ireland of Piedmont."[34]

This pessimism, however, was not entirely warranted, for the city enjoyed consistent growth. Between 1801 and 1861 the total population of Nice more than doubled, growing from less than 20,000 in 1801 to nearly 50,000 in 1861. Compared either to neighboring towns or to major French cities, Nice's growth rate was impressive (see table 2). The *hivernant* population also grew. According to estimates made by contemporaries, the number of families wintering in Nice rose from zero during the French Revolution to the pre-Revolution high of 115 families in 1815; and by 1860 about 1,000 families regularly wintered in Nice. If one accepts the not-unreasonable assumption that the average family contained 5 people, the tourist population for 1815 can be estimated at 575 persons, rising to 5,000 by 1861. Furthermore, by discounting year-to-year fluctuations and assuming a constant rate of growth in the tourist population between 1815 and 1861, a simple interpolation can be used to relate the number of tourists to the permanent population in the various census years. The results of these assumptions and derivations are shown in graph 1. If the numbers resulting from this procedure are close to the mark, there was 1 winter tourist for every 9 Niçois by 1848.[35]

These nineteenth-century visitors, following their eighteenth-century counterparts, gravitated toward the new city on the right bank of the Paillon, and it rapidly became the winter colony's preferred residence. It is hardly correct, however, to call this sprawling collection of villas and hotels a city. The Old City contained most of the businesses, although by 1860 merchants had established several shops on the right bank. The anonymous author of an early guide to Nice described the city as it existed in 1858:

> The panorama that one enjoys in Nice from the highest terraces of the château is one of the most magnificent that could be imagined: while the brown houses of the old city seem to huddle at the foot of the rock, the more charming dwellings of the new city spread out like undisciplined lambs in the vast garden which forms the plain of Nice.[36]

The English still dominated the winter colony, although many French and Russian visitors had begun wintering in the city. By 1859 Nice had fifty hotels—an increase of twenty since 1847. Those who disliked hotels and wanted to enjoy the advantages of a private dwelling constructed villas of every imaginable description. Each owner, of course, had a

TABLE 2

Population Changes in the Alpes-Maritimes, 1801–1861

City	1801	1822	% Change 1801–22	1838	% Change 1822–38	1848	% Change 1838–48	1861	% Change 1848–61	% Change 1801–61
Nice	18,475	25,831	40	33,811	31	36,804	9	48,273	31	161
Menton	3289	n.a.	....	n.a.	....	n.a.	....	4904	....	49
Sospel	2990	3620	21	4394	21	4438	1	3936	-11	32
La Brigue	2895	3300	14	3729	13	4047	9	1615*	-60*	-44*
Villefranche	2035	2491	22	2574	3	2363	-8	2911	23	43

* Reflects the population in 1858.
Source: "Dénombrement des Alpes-Maritimes" (compilation made by the Archives Départementales des Alpes-Maritimes).

different idea of what a villa should look like, and thus no thought was given to architectural harmony. Villas in styles ranging from Gothic to Byzantine to Beaux-Arts peppered the countryside. The English, especially, admired exotic styles, and their villas offended other winter residents with more conservative architectural tastes. In 1856, Prosper Mérimée, for example, bitterly attacked the English tastes in a letter to his friend Viollet-le-duc. The English, he wrote, acted like an invading army, and Mérimée found himself unable to pass one of their abominable villas without suppressing a desire to set it afire.[37]

GRAPH 1

PERMANENT POPULATION AND TOURISTS, 1801–1861

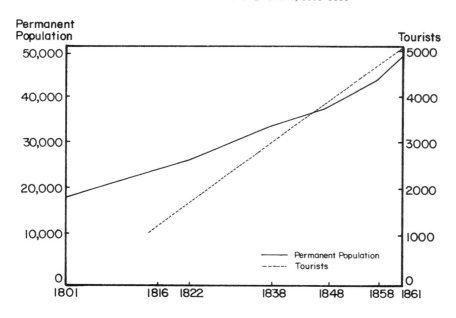

By 1860, Turin's economic abandonment of Nice and the ever-increasing numbers of visitors from the north and west convinced many Niçois that the city's future lay with France rather than Piedmont. Trade with France had increased rapidly between 1814 and 1860: by 1860 Nice bought most of its manufactured goods in France which, in turn, had become the largest consumer of Nice's main agricultural export—olive oil. Furthermore, Francophiles in Nice could argue for closer ties with France by pointing to two touchstones of nineteenth-century nationalism, "natural boundaries" and linguistic similarities. Because the main range of the Maritime Alps descends to the sea between Nice and Genoa, local Francophiles took this as a kind of divine indication that Nice was meant to be part of France. As for language, most native Niçois spoke Niçard, a dialect related to Provençal rather than to Italian. The most important factor favoring closer ties with France, however, was economic. The logic was simple: in order to prosper as a tourist city, one had to have tourists. And they were to be found in the west and north, in the cities of Britain, France, and the German states, not in the Piedmont-Sardinia or anywhere else in the Italian peninsula. Thus, for those who believed that Nice's future lay with tourism, the question was not whether Nice would become aligned with France, but how soon and how closely.[38]

These Francophiles, however, knew that it was not usual to abandon a border territory, and few French partisans could suggest methods whereby Piedmont could be persuaded to donate Nice to France. Fortunately for these partisans, two of Europe's foremost practitioners of realpolitik had secretly begun to consider the same question. On 21 July 1858, Emperor Louis Napoléon of France and Prime Minister Camilo Cavour of Piedmont-Sardinia met at Plombières (les-Bains), a spa in the Vosges. In the course of a long, private discussion Louis Napoléon agreed to furnish Piedmont with political and military support in its future attempts to conquer Austrian-held areas (particularly Venetia and Lombardy) and to give Piedmont a free hand in forming a greater kingdom of northern Italy. In return, Cavour promised to cede Nice and Savoy to France. The two leaders signed the agreement and began waiting for a satisfactory excuse to commence hostilities, as the treaty would become effective only if and when Austria committed an aggressive act.

After months of waiting, Piedmont finally managed to goad Austria into committing the required aggression. Piedmont had been mobilizing its forces, and Austria, rightly fearing that Piedmont might be planning to wage war, demanded immediate demobilization. Piedmont rejected this ultimatum on 23 April 1859, and war began. The war proceeded in a generally successful manner for France and Piedmont: the two allies defeated Austria at Magenta and Solferino, the two major battles of the war. Before Piedmont had completed its plans for the formation of a kingdom of northern Italy, however, Louis Napoléon lost his stomach for further fighting and made a separate peace with the Austrian emperor. The document, signed 11 July 1859, had the effect of transferring Lombardy to Piedmontese control. This limited victory did not fulfill the terms of the Plombières agreement, and Piedmont retained Nice and Savoy.

After a winter of reflection, Louis Napoléon began to have second thoughts about the treaty. Austrian control in northern Italy had crumbled; local leaders were demanding that their states be annexed to Piedmont. And thus, in early 1860, Cavour and Louis Napoléon agreed that Piedmont should annex Tuscany, Modena, Parma, and the Romagna and in turn France would finally receive Nice and Savoy. Napoléon insisted that, at least for the sake of appearances, the peoples involved ratify the transfers by plebiscites. Like all other Napoleonic plebiscites, these resulted in overwhelming majorities in favor of what had already been decided. (In Nice, for example, the vote was 25,743 in favor, 160 opposed, and 4,773 abstentions.)[39] Thus, for the second time in seventy years, Nice was part of France, and the city had a right to hope that the experience would be happier than that of 1792. While on a triumphal visit to Nice in August 1860, Louis Napoléon summed up the attitude of the imperial government towards its newly won city: "I do not want Nice to be able to complain that it has lost by the annexation."[40]

Indeed, most Niçois were justified in holding great expectations for the new regime. As a kind of welcoming gift to Nice, Louis Napoléon had promised to extend the Paris-Lyon-Méditerranée (P.L.M.) rail line to Nice. "Who can foresee what Nice will become," said Mayor Malaussána, "when the railroad puts [the city] in communication with the main lines of the interior and with all the great cities of civilized Europe?" Not long ago, he noted, the people of Nice believed that extending the railroad to their city was only a dream, the accomplishment of which seemed reserved for future generations; now, because of the solicitude of the emperor, one could hope to see tracks at the banks of the Var before the end of 1862. Naturally, once the trip from Calais or Paris could be made entirely by rail, this would mean a greater influx of visitors.[41]

Thus, by 1860 Nice was well on its way to becoming a full-fledged tourist city. It had developed a sizable infrastructure of hotels, restaurants, shops, and entertainment facilities. Nice's municipal leaders understood that the city's future lay in its ability to attract visitors, and they recognized the need for municipal investments in streets, promenades, and municipal facilities. Most important, Nice had gained an asset no tourist center can do without—a reputation. The city had become known throughout the aristocratic worlds of France and Britain as a place to be seen, and in some circles a visit to Nice had become a natural step for anyone in imperfect health. Yet Nice also faced grave problems which had to be solved if the brilliant future that some predicted for it were ever to become a reality. The most pressing problem was still communications. Although the basic outline of the French railway system was nearly complete by 1860, Marseilles was still the closest railroad terminal. Nice's hopes for the future would be seriously compromised if Louis Napoléon's promise of a rail link was not fulfilled. Second, Nice was faced with making massive investments to improve its appearance and wholesomeness. After all, reasoned the more forward-looking Niçois, how could the wealthiest and most demanding people in Europe be expected to visit a city whose facilities remained those of a Piedmontese village? Finally, a few realized that an economy based solely on tourism would catalyze many human problems involving the relationships between the local population and the visitors.

2

Planning, Development, and the Urban Environment

IN THE SECOND HALF OF THE NINETEENTH CENTURY, following France's annexation of Nice, the Niçois found themselves caught up in a cycle of municipal development that astonished even the city's most enthusiastic boosters. Becoming part of imperial France promised a new and bright future for the city and for its tourist industry. The prospect of rail links with cosmopolitan Europe meant that visitors could travel to and from the city with relative ease. Furthermore, the elimination of customs and police barriers for visitors arriving from the north and west meant easy entry into Nice. As part of his efforts to convince the Niçois that the switch to French nationality had been a wise one, Louis Napoléon encouraged investment in the city, a policy that injected much-needed capital into Nice. Finally, the general and rapid expansion of industry and commerce throughout Europe meant that investors were accumulating money at a rapid rate; many of the newly rich used their wealth to purchase one of the greatest luxuries available—a winter spent on the Riviera.

Taken together, these political and economic changes dictated a period of growth and expansion for Nice. With the exception of a sharp depression caused by the Franco-Prussian War (1870-71), Nice's economy expanded during the next two decades, and money flowed into the city as never before. Much of this wealth was speculative in nature—investors did not interest themselves so much in a steady return on capital as they did in rising land prices that would permit rapid and profitable resale. Real estate prices ballooned so quickly that they soon bore little relationship to the income that might result from the use of the land. No one knew when the bubble would burst, and land buyers and builders continued to buy and sell in the classic manner, assuming that prices would rise indefinitely. The result was predictable—villas, apartments, and hotels sprang up like tropical flowers on the right bank of the Paillon. This spectacular rate of growth, and the extraordinary speculative profits that resulted from it, led to a sense of complacency in the minds of civic leaders and citizens alike. Nice's public officials were unable to consider the growth of their city in a leisurely fashion, were unwilling to take any actions that might retard or halt the city's prosperity, and were committed to laissez-faire economics. These officials generally avoided planning or controlling the shape and appearance of the city. Thus, under their benign leadership, most decisions concerning the use of land, the type and style of constructions, and the relationship of buildings to streets and public places were made privately by builders and developers. They directed the shape of the city during the crucial stage of growth, when Nice became known as "the living room of Europe" and "the queen of the Riviera," a time when the city also became the captive of its tourist industry.

The event that aroused most hope in the hearts of Nice's business elite was Louis Napoléon's postannexation promise of rail links between Nice and Paris. The French rail network had grown rapidly since 1850, and the railway company that operated in the southeast, the P.L.M., had become one of France's strongest and most prosperous.[1] It came into existence in 1852 when the three small companies operating in the Rhône Valley merged. That same year the new conglomerate received permission to build a line connecting Marseilles and Toulon. The P.L.M. put the Marseilles-to-Toulon connection into service on 3 May 1859, and on 3 August 1859, three weeks after the signing of the Treaty of Villafranca, rail construction to the Var was authorized. A year later, after the annexation of Nice became official, the P.L.M. received authorization to complete a line linking the Var to Nice.[2] The imperial government, anxious to bind its newly won territory to France as rapidly as possible, actively encouraged the work, and the P.L.M. completed the first section (Toulon to Solliès-Pont) in December 1861. By 10 May 1863, track had been laid to Cannes, and by 10 August of the same year the line had been pushed to the Var. The technical problems involved in bridging the Var retarded the P.L.M.'s ultimate arrival in Nice, and the last section was not finished until late in 1864.[3]

While local residents joyfully received the news that the emperor's promise of rail connections would be fulfilled, the coming of the railroad forced the city to consider its future more seriously than it ever had before. If Nice were to have a railroad, it would have to have a station. Although all could agree on this, no such unanimity existed concerning the site of the station. The arguments that emerged about its proper location are useful in understanding how various local interest groups perceived the city's future development.

The basic question posed by the coming of the railway was one that sharply divided Nice: Did the city's future lie with tourism or with commerce and trade? Although Nice had never been a major trading center in the past, its new political ties and its improved transportation facilities promised a bright commercial future, particularly when Nice's new status as a favored imperial city was taken into account. Those who saw Nice as a potentially great commercial center argued that the station should be located on the left bank of the Paillon as close to the harbor as possible so that merchandise could easily be transferred between ships and freight cars. With this capability, they felt, Nice would soon become a major Mediterranean port, and could possibly even rival Marseilles. Nice's traditional commercial establishment favored this solution because it would boost the city's small but venerable import-export business.

Opposing the left-bank site were those who believed that Nice's economic future was inextricably tied to tourism. This group favored a location that would facilitate the arrival and departure of visitors. France, they argued, had no need for another Mediterranean port; and they laughed at the idea that Nice, with its tiny man-made harbor, would ever be able to compete with Marseilles or Toulon. They believed that Nice's station should be located far from the Old City so that arriving visitors would be struck at once with the beauty of the Bay of Angels and Nice's villa-studded basin. Also, a station located on the right bank of the Paillon would be closer to the Croix-de-Marbre area, where most visitors preferred to stay.[4]

The debate over where to locate the station was heated, both in the municipal council and among the general public. One member of the municipal council asked the mayor to verify a rumor that the P.L.M. had not received permission from the Ministery of Public Works to cross the Paillon, making a left-bank site impossible. The rumor, Mayor François Malausséna admitted, was true. The council could express a preference for the left-bank station if it so desired, the mayor said, but in his opinion such action would be neither "opportune nor advisable." In fact, the site had already been chosen by the P.L.M., without any official consultation with local representatives. As at Plombières, a decision crucial to Nice's future had been made far from the city without public notice or regard for local opinions. The terminal was a dead-end; no tracks headed east from the station. Furthermore, as Nice's commercial establishment soon learned, the P.L.M. did not intend to build any large-scale freight-handling facilities or feeder lines that would connect the station to the port. The P.L.M. and the imperial government had presented Nice with a fait accompli. Nice's future, they had apparently decided, lay with tourism rather than trade. The decision to build the railroad without regard for Nice's shipping community inextricably bound the city's future to tourism. Rails would cross the Paillon only when and if the time came to extend the line to Italy.[5]

The remaining question concerned the precise placement of the city's railroad terminal. Barriers such as highways or railroad tracks always determine urban patterns of growth, and Nice's leaders realized that locating the terminal in virgin territory would inevitably form a ring within which the city would have to grow. They generally agreed that the station should be placed on or near the axis of the future avenue du Prince Impérial. The major controversy concerned the station's distance from the sea. Some, including many members of the municipal council, thought that the terminal should be a mere 700 meters from the sea, while others argued that if the station was at least 1,500 meters inland, the noise and smoke from the trains would never intrude on the tourist quarters. Eventually, in a compromise move, the P.L.M. and the city agreed to locate the station 900 meters from the sea and 200 meters west of the avenue du Prince Impérial (see map 1).

The arguments over the terminal's location shed considerable light on the city's understanding of its role as a tourist center and its perception of the kind of visitors it was likely to attract. Most Niçois assumed that their future guests would be similar to the typical eighteenth-century visitors who had come to Nice in search of peace, repose, and sunlight. Local leaders thought that these tourists would arrive at the station, go by carriage to their hotels or villas, and have no further need for rail transportation until their departure in the spring. With this scenario, it made sense to locate the station as far from existing hotels and villas as possible, minimizing the impact of soot, smoke, and noise. On the other hand, if visitors were transients who would remain in Nice only for a few days, the station logically should have been sited closer to the commercial quarter, serving the needs of shippers and merchants as well as tourists. The decision to place the station on an agricultural prairie 900 meters from the sea was a clear victory for those who saw Nice as a center for sun-and-air *villégiature*. Away from the city's tourist-oriented suburbs, the station would be unobtrusive. Trains would bring visitors to the city but would not annoy them after their arrival. Thus situated, the railroad was not much use to Nice's traditional business community, but it was ideal for the *hivernants* and those who served them.[6]

After the basic siting decisions had been made, the P.L.M. quickly extended its lines from the Var to the city; on 18 October 1864, the first train pulled into Nice. It is impossible to overestimate the impact of the railroad on the city—and indeed on the development of the whole French Riviera. For the first time a traveler could leave Paris for Nice,

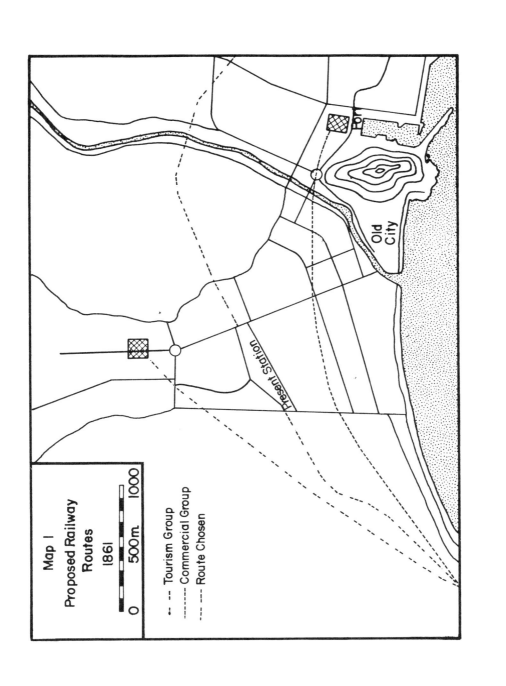

Map 1
Proposed Railway
Routes

1861

0   500m.   1000

--- Tourism Group
---- Commercial Group
--- Route Chosen

Present Station

Old
City

Port

secure in the knowledge that he would arrive at a stated time, without having to encounter such unpleasant surprises as flooded rivers, unavailable coaches, or washed-out roads. He also could take advantage of dramatically increased speed which by 1869 allowed him to travel from London to Paris in ten hours and forty minutes and from Paris to Marseilles in seventeen hours.[7] By 1875 a voyager could leave London at 7:40 A.M. and have supper in Nice the next evening. Compared to the prerail period, the change was revolutionary. Indeed, completion of the railway "launched" Nice and, by linking the city to Europe, hurled the sleepy Mediterranean resort into the modern world. As one scholar has noted, "Until 1860 to mark Nice's place in French literature is a difficult research problem; since 1860 it is a problem of elimination."[8]

Although both Nice's leaders and the officers of the P.L.M. knew that the new rail connections between Nice and Toulon would generate some traffic, no one could accurately estimate how many passengers were likely to go to Nice, the end of the line. It soon became clear, however, that any fears the P.L.M. may have had regarding low passenger loads were unfounded. Between 1865 (the first full year of P.L.M.'s operation in Nice) and 1874 the total number of passengers nearly tripled, rising from 106,341 in 1865 to 309,779 in 1874.[9] This meant that on the average, there were 291 arrivals per day in 1865 and 849 per day in 1874 (see graph 2). These figures are particularly impressive because they include no travelers merely passing through Nice. Even after the rail lines were extended into Italy in 1872, there were few transients because Italian intercity connections were still in a primitive stage.[10]

It is, of course, impossible to separate tourists from those traveling for commercial or personal reasons. Furthermore, although rail links into Italy did not exist until 1872, the P.L.M. did establish a highly successful line between Nice and Monaco in 1868; some of the increase in traffic in 1868–69 reflects the movement of gamblers who commuted from Nice to the Monte Carlo casino in Monaco. Nevertheless, one general conclusion can be drawn from these figures. Taken as a whole, the 1860s saw an enormous increase in total tourist traffic as a direct result of the new railroad connections.

It is much more difficult to determine the exact size of the winter colony during the decade following 1865. While everyone in Nice knew that the city's economy advanced and receded with the winter colony, no one in this prestatistical age cared to count the visitors systematically. Thus, the only numbers available are the impressionistic observations of those who chanced to write essays or books about winter life in Nice. These authors reported that the winter colony grew from about 4,000 *hivernants* in 1861 to around 33,000 in 1881. This is more than a sevenfold increase, and it closely parallels the changes in railroad traffic. Indeed, as graph 2 shows, the number of *hivernants* increased in proportion to total arrivals. Although one should not place too much emphasis on this covariance, the ratio of winterers to arrivals (about 1:12) is probably meaningful enough to use, in the absence of any other data, to roughly estimate the number of *hivernants* in a particular year. Clearly

GRAPH 2

ARRIVALS BY RAIL AND WINTERERS, 1861–1881

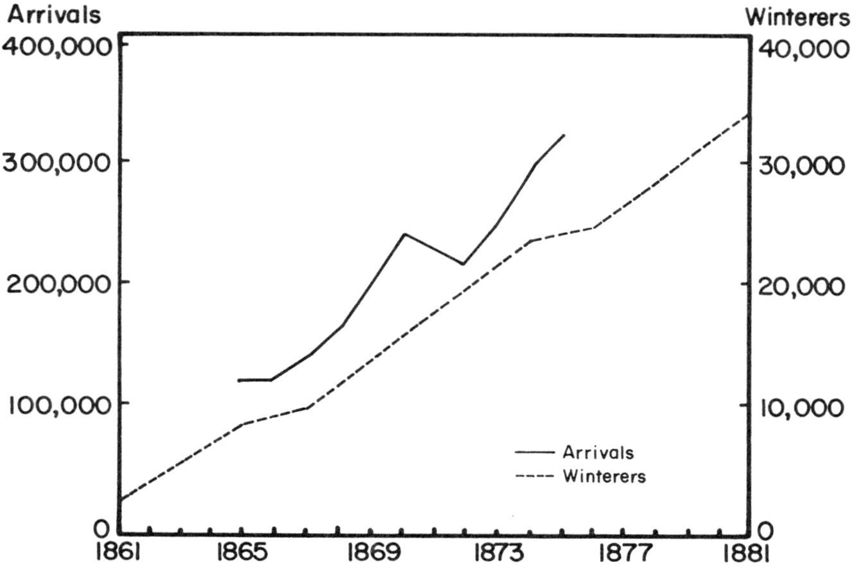

the number of visitors wintering in Nice during this period increased dramatically. The only dip in the rate of growth came during the Franco-Prussian War. Few foreigners cared to visit Nice then, due to the unstable political climate in France; and few Frenchmen were able to think about *villégiature* while the Germans besieged their capital and occupied much of the country. The "terrible year," as 1870–71 was called, while not as devastating to Nice as it was to Paris, virtually bankrupted the Mediterranean city. "It is unfortunately all too true," said a municipal councilor, "that our working class is suffering; the war has stopped building, has stopped the movement of travelers, has kept away foreigners, and has thus led to the impoverishment of all those who live by their labor."[11]

The lesson of the Franco-Prussian War—that Nice's economic-well-being depended entirely on tourism—was forcefully expressed by Nice's mayor Auguste Raynaud, who led the city from 1871 to 1878. In his valedictory address Raynaud eloquently pointed out to his council just how dependent Nice had become on the fruits of tourism. He began by citing the city's evident prosperity which was reflected by the receipts from the tax of 24.5 centimes per franc levied on the assessed value of real and personal property. The revenue from this tax had risen from 115,300 francs in 1868 (Nice's most prosperous year under the Second Empire) to 180,991 francs in 1877—an increase of 57 percent. At the same time, however, noted Raynaud, those activities that had tradition-ally formed Nice's economic base were in a state of decline: agricultural production had collapsed, and many farmers had abandoned unprofitable land; maritime activity had slowed to a crawl; perfume factories were disappearing; silk spinning had died out; and many other small industries were in great distress. The only explanation for Nice's obvious prosperity was the rapid growth of the foreign colony and the development of commercial and agricultural activities dependent on it. "We must congratulate ourselves all the more," said Raynaud, "because this source of prosperity is the only one in our city which has not dried up." Fur-thermore, he noted, no improvement in general commerce could be foreseen. The city had been unable to enlarge its port, and the P.L.M. had again refused to consider constructing a maritime rail station near the port.[12] In 1879 an assistant to the new mayor, Alfred Borriglione, wrote, "We have in our city neither mills, nor factories, nor industries, nor mines," adding, "here are only several workshops of little impor-tance."[13] Three years later, a newspaper catering to the foreign colony could gloat that foreign visitors "are the principal, if not the only resource of the area."[14]

Although most Niçois enjoyed the wealth that the winter colony brought to the city, Nice's dependence on tourism had several potentially dangerous side effects—in particular, the development of a service-oriented labor force. As workers left the declining traditional areas—agriculture, commerce, and maritime activities—and as new workers came to Nice searching for employment, the work force became more and more concentrated in tourist-related occupations. In general, this meant that two basic groupings dominated the occupational structure of Nice: those who directly served the visitors by working as domestic servants or as hotel, restaurant, and entertainment employees and those who served the visitors' indirect needs by working in all parts of the construction industry. The second group rapidly became the mainstay of Nice's labor force. As early as 1862 observers were struck with Nice's housing boom. The prefect of Alpes-Maritimes, Denis Gavini de Campile, wrote at the beginning of the 1862 season that the city expected so many rich families "that the business of renting apartments, already so prosperous last year, seems bound to expand in spite of the fact that over 200 large buildings have been built since last year."[15]

A Rural Villa Designed by the Architect Vaudremer, c. 1880 *(courtesy of the Bibliothèque National, Paris)*

Although information detailing the exact number of dwellings built each year in Nice is not available, some inferences can be drawn from an examination of the tax on doors and windows *(portes-et-fenêtres)* in Nice and in Alpes-Maritimes.[16] This tax was based on the assumption that the number of openings in a dwelling reflected the prosperity within. Like other nineteenth-century French taxes, it protected the privacy of the taxpayer: officials could make all assessments without either entering the interior of a home or prying into personal affairs. The door-and-window tax was thus a combined measure of the number of dwellings in a given place and of the level of prosperity of its residents. Receipts in Nice showed a steady and pronounced rate of growth during the years immediately following 1860; the assessed valuation in the Department of Alpes-Maritimes grew from 113,303 francs in 1861 to 259,208 francs in 1885 to 354,962 francs in 1904. In addition, the per capita number of doors and windows also increased in the city of Nice. By 1872 Nice possessed 2.27 doors and windows for each person; in 1881 this ratio was 2.64. These figures are striking when compared to the French national average of 1.5 doors and windows per person throughout the period. Several factors could explain Nice's statistics. First, the per capita number of doors and windows obviously would increase as buildings became more luxurious. Second, the per capita figure would also increase as the rate of building outpaced the growth of the population. A third explanation, of course, was that Nice's official census figures were too low, an explanation favored by local officials, who were unwilling to recognize the possibility that the city was becoming overbuilt. In retrospect, however, it appears that the first and second possibilities are more plausible, particularly when one takes into account data provided by the Bureau de l'Enregistrement.[17]

The receipts of this office, which was responsible for recording and taxing all transactions of real and intangible property, rose from slightly over 2 million francs in 1877 to nearly 5.3 million francs in 1881, an increase of 159 percent. To be sure, the transfer of nonreal property accounted for a certain proportion of these receipts, but this proportion was relatively small. In general these numbers can be taken as a gauge of activity in the buying and selling of real estate. Construction was booming, and the real estate market was flourishing at a rate that must have seemed extraordinary to Niçois who had come of age during the sleepy, prerail, Sardinian years.[18]

So many people were employed in the city's construction industry that Nice's municipal leaders tended to encourage building and rapid development with all the means at their disposal. Planning, which carried with it the possibility that growth might be retarded, became more difficult, and the possible negative consequences of over-building were seldom considered. In 1872, for example, during a municipal discussion focusing on ways in which the city administration could stimulate construction and thus increase employment, an iconoclastic council member observed that the rate of construction in Nice had already expanded far beyond the needs of either its permanent or its transient population.

Mayor Raynaud recognized the point, but replied that one should not "forget the fact that the construction industry is the only one that proceeds with any success in Nice and that until other industries capable of rendering the same services are established, it is essential to encourage the one that provides work for the largest part of the working class." The prefect Albert Decrais wrote in his annual report for 1875 that "in Nice, and in the other towns of the littoral and the department, where the main objective of the residents is to attract foreigners, the construction of buildings continues to soar more and more markedly."[19] Indeed, when the depression of the 1880s struck Nice and construction came to a standstill, much of the city's labor force was obliged to seek work elsewhere.

Impressed by the construction-inspired prosperity, Nice's municipal council usually actively encouraged building. Although most of its power was indirect, the council could effect the rate and style of construction by manipulating the codes that governed the use of land in the city. By approving or denying requests to depart from building regulations, by opening streets, and by providing municipal services, the council could do much to guide Nice's expansion. The most important tool by which the city administration could shape Nice's growth, however, was the application (or nonapplication) of the city's master plan (*plan régulateur*). By developing and interpreting these plans the council could, if it wished, control how builders used the land and—most important to Nice's entrepreneurial community—its market value.

The municipal administration had been actively involved in urban planning since the old Consiglio d'Ornato was established in 1832. The Consiglio had developed several successive plans designed to regulate the growth of Nice during what it considered to be the foreseeable future. It had focused, therefore, almost exclusively on two areas: that bordering the Paillon and opposite the Old City (the area known as St.-Jean-Baptiste); and the strip of land paralleling the route de France called Longchamp or the Croix-de-Marbre—the area most favored by Nice's early winter visitors. Between 1832 and 1860, the Consiglio had labored long and hard to avoid the disorder and confusion which it considered to be the inevitable result of unregulated growth. Its members' hatred of disorder caused them to depend heavily on straight lines when laying out streets, and they were largely responsible for imposing a grid pattern on these two areas.[20]

The Sardinian government revised and expanded the original 1832 plan. The 1858 revision is important as it laid out the basic design of most of Nice's major streets in the areas between the sea and what was then called the *boulevards d'enceinte* ("belt boulevards"), the band of major streets between the railway and the sea (see map 2).[21] Besides their general conviction that streets aligned at right angles were best, the early planners had two practical reasons for establishing a gridiron. First, they wanted the streets to be at ninety degree angles to the prevailing winds to aid in ventilation. Second, they wanted the buildings that would border the broad streets paralleling the Paillon and the sea to have maximum exposure to the sun on the southeast and the southwest. This second requirement was particularly important because all those who visited Nice in search of better health insisted on renting sunny apartments and were willing to pay premium prices for them.[22]

Although generally satisfactory from a technical point of view, the 1858 plan had one serious defect: it did not anticipate the need for transversal streets, and often the placement of these streets was left to the discretion of landowners.[23] A glance at a street map of Nice shows many relatively broad streets that parallel the sea and the Paillon and many cross streets that seem to have been placed capriciously, at every conceivable angle.

When control of Nice passed from Piedmont-Sardinia to France in 1860, the city's property owners, hoping that the new regime would be less severe in applying the master plan, challenged it immediately. In May 1861, the council received its first request for a variance in the construction requirements dictated by the 1858 plan. M. Arnouse, owner of a large four-story building located on the square at the mouth of the Paillon, asked the council to allow him to add a fifth story to his building. Like many other proprietors, Arnouse believed that the change in regimes had dissolved the requirements made by the Consiglio d'Ornato and that property owners no longer had to follow the Sardinian regulations. The municipal council felt otherwise and argued that

> the ever-increasing influx of families which come here to stay for a
> portion of the year and which, for the most part, have adopted habits
> of comfort, elegance, and luxury during stays in the great capitals of
> Europe, requires that in certain quarters, questions of alignment, regu-
> larity, and charm should be placed among those of the first order.[24]

The municipal council ruled that the owners of buildings built under the Sardinian regime did not have the right to ignore the regulations made by the Consiglio d'Ornato. Existing buildings, or those under construction in 1860, could be changed only with the approval of the municipal council, the prefect, and the appropriate minister in Paris. Those who attempted to lift the dead hand of the Consiglio met with mixed results. Each request for a variance was reviewed individually; some were granted and most were not. The only way a property owner could circumvent the system was to build illegally and hope that the

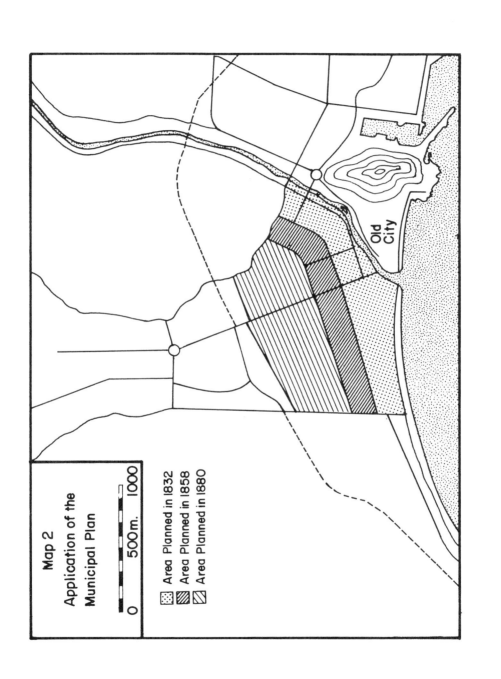

Map 2
Application of the
Municipal Plan

0   500m.   1000

▦ Area Planned in 1832
▨ Area Planned in 1858
▧ Area Planned in 1880

Old
City

illicit alterations would go unnoticed for thirty years, the statute of limitations for such offenses. The imperial government's support of the Sardinian plan, coupled with the Malausséna administration's distaste for variances, kept requests for changes at a minimum.[25]

Underlying this lack of attempts to circumvent the master plan was the broad, general acceptance that the work of the Consiglio d'Ornato had received throughout Nice. Besides achieving the goal of giving the city a grid pattern of streets and assuring that traffic would move with relative ease, the master plan had had the important side effect of dramatically increasing the value of land included in it. After the revision of 1858, for example, land bordering the projected streets in both the Croix-de-Marbre and the St.-Jean-Baptiste quarters rapidly rose in value, often doubling or tripling. Land that previously could not be sold at any price suddenly commanded a premium. "There," remarked one councilor, "one sees palaces and villas rise like magic on lots that before the master plan were only fields or vegetable gardens."[26] The potential value of planned land was so obvious that many landowners began aligning parcels outside the master plan with it in hopes that future official plans would include their private roads. Indeed, the value of land was so dependent on the application of the master plan that the least indication that it would not be followed tended to decrease the rate of land sales. Capitalists, observed Mayor Malausséna, would not want to invest their funds in developing lots that might become inaccessible in the future. In his opinion, "The future of the city of Nice which has been called to spread over the right bank depends absolutely on the strict application of the master plan."[27]

This is not to say that planners and landowners were always in agreement. In a city like Nice where land speculation had become a way of life, conflict was inevitable whenever a planning decision had to be made: a prime example was the controversy surrounding the major artery that would connect the new railroad station to the city. The first question facing local leaders concerned the direction that the avenue de la Gare should take after crossing the railroad tracks.[28] According to the Consiglio d'Ornato's original plan, the street was to extend in a straight line into the plain north of Nice. The street was not constructed, however, before the completion of rail links. The arrival of the railway and the general expansion that followed made this area more attractive for villa construction and focused intense attention on plans for the street. In April 1864 a group of landowners petitioned the municipal council to have the street's direction changed so that it would angle off to the east, passing through their holdings. Their motives were purely pecuniary—they hoped that the street would increase the value of their land. They were gambling that land north of the railway would become attractive to *hivernants*—a reasonable assumption in 1864, but still a gamble. The landowners, however, had sufficient confidence in the future of this area to present a petition to the mayor offering to donate to the city all the land required for the proposed deviation and to provide a construction subsidy of 12,000 francs (later raised to 20,400 francs). Nice's municipal councilors felt that they could not ignore this offer, master plan or no, and immediately ordered a study of the proposal and its cost. The engineers decided that because the city would not have to condemn much land to follow the eastward route, a considerable amount of money could be saved by accepting the landowners' offer. The less farsighted landowners whose property lay in the street's original path had refused to give the city a subvention or to cede any land, despite the fact that, in principle, most councilors favored the direct route. Eventually, a year later, these landowners did offer both free land and a subsidy, but by then it was too late: the municipal council had made its decision.[29]

A later major decision concerning the avenue de la Gare was much more significant for the style of the city as it concerned the width and appearance of this major artery between the sea and the railroad tracks. Originally, the Consiglio d'Ornato's plan called for this street to be fourteen meters wide with broad sidewalks of six meters on either side. In addition, the store-fronts were to have arcades, much like those on the rue de Rivoli in Paris. Le comte de Grandchamp, chief engineer of the Department of Alpes-Maritimes, modified the plan somewhat by eliminating the arcades, but he approved the grand approach. He suggested that the avenue have a main lane of ten meters, two frontage roads of eight meters each, and sidewalks of two and a half meters each. He also recommended that the buildings bordering the street be placed seven meters back from the sidewalks and that this intervening space contain ornamental plants. "It is necessary," he was quoted as saying,

> that the glances of strollers only encounter gardens planted with flowers. Only under this condition will inhabitants come to draw the greatest benefits possible from their climate and from a sky which, if I may say so, is without rival in Europe. . . . The avenue du Prince Impérial [as the avenue de la Gare was then called], featuring two sidewalks protected all along the pavement by hedges of roses and oleanders and planted on each side with two lines of plantaines, will become the most agreeable and the most used promenade in Nice.[30]

Although the city council accepted this report in January 1865, local business forces soon caused a reversal. The owners of property along the street were incensed. They thought that the idea of setting shops back seven meters from the street was ridiculous, expensive, and bad for business because it would make it difficult for customers to enter their stores. The implicit threat, of course, was that these landowners would force the city to pay them enormous sums for the land taken up by the street, walks, and borders. (Usually, owners either ceded the land or asked only small indemnities for it in anticipation of its escalating value.) The city's last ditch efforts to obtain subsidies from Paris for the wide and luxurious avenue failed: in late 1865 the minister of public works informed the council that the central government would not under-write condemnation expenses or help defray construction costs. Thus, with regret, the council abandoned its plans to build either a rue de Rivoli or an avenue des Champs Elysées and instead settled for an avenue de la Gare.[31]

The way in which the municipal council approached the land-use problems surrounding development of the avenue de la Gare illustrates several fundamental conditions that were to shape Nice's future as a tourist town. First, the decision not to build a magnificent ornamental boulevard suggests a basic ambivalence regarding Nice's future. No matter how successful the tourist industry became, many Niçois retained a healthy scepticism toward it and refused to allow themselves to become too dependent on it. They knew that war or international crisis could abruptly halt travel to Nice; prosperity could end; and, disaster of disasters, the visitors could simply decide not to come to Nice any more. If any of these possibilities materialized, a grand boulevard, forty-five meters wide, built through open fields would be the ultimate absurdity, and those scoffers who had never believed that tourism could support a city would have a field day.

Second, the controversy illustrates the fact that in 1865, the municipality seemed unsure of the degree to which it should commit itself and the municipal treasury in an effort to attract and retain visitors. Nearly everyone could agree that certain basic investments had to be made—the streets had to be built, some attention had to be paid to building and maintaining streets and promenades, and some effort had to be made to furnish Nice with municipal services. Beyond this, however, there was considerable uncertainty as to how far the city should extend its resources. Different opinions, of course, were related to one's faith in the long-term future of Nice as a tourist city. If the city fathers could have known that Nice would almost triple in size between 1866 and 1911 (growing from a city of some 50,000 souls to a metropolis of over 142,000), they quite likely would have made the investment required to turn the avenue de la Gare into an avenue des Champs Elysées. This kind of perspicacity, however, is given to few, and the municipal council had legitimate doubts about how much city money they should commit to a project that would be more decorative than utilitarian. The municipal council knew it should build a street, but it did not know if its role included building a monument.

Third, arguments over construction of the avenue de la Gare illustrate the shifting balance that existed between the desires of builders and those of planners. Everyone in Nice wanted to accommodate the demands of the tourists who, in the 1870s and early '80s, insisted on habitations that were calm, surrounded by open space, and easily accessible. The question was whether this kind of bucolic environment could best be achieved by imposing a predetermined pattern on the city or by allowing Nice to grow organically, with its style and pattern governed by day-to-day, individual decisions. This conflict, common to modern cities, was particularly acute in Nice after the annexation in 1860 because growth proceeded so rapidly. In Nice the solutions to this conflict seemed to depend heavily on economic conditions. When demand for new construction was particularly heavy, planners took a back seat and allowed entrepreneurs to build as they wished within certain basic guidelines. When the economy slowed, the planners would regroup, blame the slowdown on a lack of planning during the boom period, and proceed to create elegant designs for the future. These plans, however, seldom included enough land to encompass the next period of growth, and once expansion began again, the cycle would start anew. The map of Nice reflects this combination of private and public urban planning: the more regular quarters were generally created during periods of economic stagnation; the less regular quarters generally date from boom years, when most seemed to agree that irregular quarters were a small price to pay for the prosperity helped along by speculative building. The tendency of the city to outgrow its plan became evident soon after Nice became part of France. Both the quarter St.-Jean-Baptiste and the quarter Croix-de-Marbre experienced such rapid development after 1860 that one of the city's most pressing tasks was to regulate construction in these areas. Uncertainty as to whether the entire area between the sea and the railway would become part of the city complicated the problem. Unwilling to take steps that might harm the post-annexation prosperity, Nice's administration did nothing—a course of action which made the eventual construction of regularly spaced streets impossible.

The demands of Nice's visitors also helped undermine the master plan. Those wealthy members of Europe's aristocracy and upper bourgeoisie who chose to spend their winters in Nice came because it offered the best of two worlds: one could enjoy the peace and sunshine of a country villa while being close enough to the city proper to enjoy its distractions whenever one wished. Those who visited Nice during the winter, and whose money fueled the construction boom, had very little of what might be called an essential urban connection—that is, their day-to-day contacts with the city were severely limited, and they had few commitments to it. The winter residents did not work in Nice; they had no family ties there; and they usually chose their friends from their own group. In a sense these visitors viewed Nice as a kind of artificial community, much as modern Americans view sun-belt retirement centers. The *hivernants* were willing to spend large sums in the city, but in return they demanded access to the Riviera sun, plentiful entertainment facilities, wholesome surroundings, and a generally calm and salubrious environment.

The desire to be of, but not in, the city had important consequences for Nice's growth and development. In general, the preannexation housing pattern continued after 1860 with the tourist population being divided into two groups: a minority preferred hotel accommodations, and the majority purchased or rented villas or cottages. As the popularity of Nice increased after 1860, the proportion of visitors who were willing to invest in villas increased. The consequence was that land on the outskirts of Nice rapidly became peppered with private villas, located purely in accordance with the whims of the owner or builder. There was no reason why they should have been sited otherwise—the areas in which these villas were constructed were far from the perimeter of the master plan, and few builders of villas ever thought that the city would expand that much. However, there was such rapid growth during the second half of the nineteenth century that land once beyond the city limits, occupied by villas and their gardens, often was annexed.

The villa owners were Nice's most dependable *hivernants,* and since their money was required to keep the local economy moving, few land-use decisions could be made without considering their desires. These visitors, however, were not interested in Nice as a functioning city in the same sense an office worker or laborer was. The winter residents did not worry about living in proximity to a workplace; they were wealthy enough to be able to ignore the economic advantages of multiple-family dwellings; and they seldom had family or social connections that would have made living near the center of the city desirable. As a result, many of the visitors demanded individual houses, surrounded by garden space, far from the city center.

Thus, Nice's housing pattern differed significantly from most other Western cities. During the last half of the nineteenth century, nearly every important city in Europe and North America experienced sig-

The Winter Quarter of Carabacel, c. 1870 (courtesy of the Bibliothèque National, Paris)

nificant suburban development. Most of this expansion resulted from the arrival of residents who depended on the city for their livelihoods and who merely enjoyed residing in the relatively uncrowded suburbs. They still retained their essential connection to the city, and progressive suburban growth depended largely on the availability of transportation to and from the city center. This meant that the suburbs which sprang up around industrial or commercial cities were forced by nineteenth-century circumstances—such as the proximity of trams, trolleys, or rails—to develop in disciplined patterns.[32] As H. J. Dyos noted in studying the London suburb of Camberwell, "If cheap fares had helped to fill up the inner suburbs . . . the lack of adequate transport had left others half empty."[33]

In Nice, on the other hand, suburbs developed according to different imperatives. The availability of public transportation had little to do with the city's rapid growth after 1860 because there was none, other than cabs. Only in 1880 did a miserable, two-line horse-drawn tramway system appear, and the century was over before a superior tram became available.[34] Thus, the main force governing development in Nice was the universal demand of the *hivernants* for sunshine, gardens, and open spaces, coupled with the landowners' desire to make their properties both as attractive and as remunerative as possible. In practice, this meant that the villas destined for *hivernants* were widely dispersed, surrounded with gardens (and often walls), and assumed no order except for that provided by the boundaries of land parcels.

The main problem with this for the city was the difficulty in applying logical street plans to areas already occupied by villas and their ornamental gardens. Nevertheless, the rate of construction in the area made the establishment of some kind of planning absolutely essential if total chaos were to be avoided. So in 1880, instead of continuing the street pattern established in the 1858 master plan, the municipal council decided, first, to build new streets in accordance with the property lines in the area and, second, to integrate into the plan pre-existing private roads that already had villas built along them. This compromise had several advantages: it did not antagonize owners of villas; it avoided costly condemnation and indemnification; and it did not slow construction by forcing builders to face an uncertain future. The new plan disturbed few houses and generally did not break up land parcels—a feature that kept property values high. Paths separating lots and driveways often were declared official streets. This practice guaranteed a chaotic street alignment and insured that the suburbs that had grown up during the 1870s would soon be extremely congested once the land began to be used for businesses and multi-family dwellings. This, however, was deemed to be a minor irritant when compared with the problems accompanying the disruption of both construction and growth; the interests of landowners had to be protected. "We must not forget," said the municipal councilor charged with presenting the new 1880 master plan, "that in drawing streets on the plan which cannot be built immediately, we make the position of property owners excessively weak because they would be forced to follow a plan from which they would not be able to profit."[35] In short, planning that did not follow the pattern of development could destroy Nice's prosperity (see map 3).

The effects of this approach are clearly visible on a map of Nice: the quarters aligned by the Sardinian municipal administration during a period of relative stability can be easily spotted in comparison to those laid out after Nice's economy began to boom. The early Sardinian approaches to planning are evident, for example, in the quarter of St.-Jean-Baptiste. Its alignment was the result of successively more complex plans from 1832 to 1858.[36] The area between the 1858 alignment and the railroad tracks, however, received no attention from the Sardinians and only benefited from the master plan of 1880, adopted long after the need for it became obvious; the results of this delay are seen in the pattern of its streets. The contrast between these two quarters illustrates a significant difference in outlook between the two regimes and reflects as well the differing economic conditions under which each operated.

The extreme regularity of streets in the quarter of St.-Jean-Baptiste illustrates the emphasis that the Sardinian Consiglio d'Ornato placed on planning in anticipation of growth, so as to avoid disorder. All construction had to be approved by the Consiglio, and no builder was allowed to violate the Consiglio's views of regularity. The frequent revisions of the master plan and the willingness to include land far from the city's perimeter illustrate the Consiglio's dedication to regularity.

The French regime, however, dedicated to a laissez-faire approach to urban planning, tended to put aside questions of alignment for as long as possible and showed little interest in anticipating future construction. Thus, by the time the French authorities began developing their own master plan in 1879, there was no possibility of applying it to the quarters where it was most needed without destroying hundreds of villas and endangering the financial health of many landowners. The municipal council's decision to officially adopt as streets those lines of communication that had evolved in the natural course of land development was the cheapest and most politically popular action possible. These administrators, more concerned with growth than regularity, were willing to let construction and land development evolve without being overly

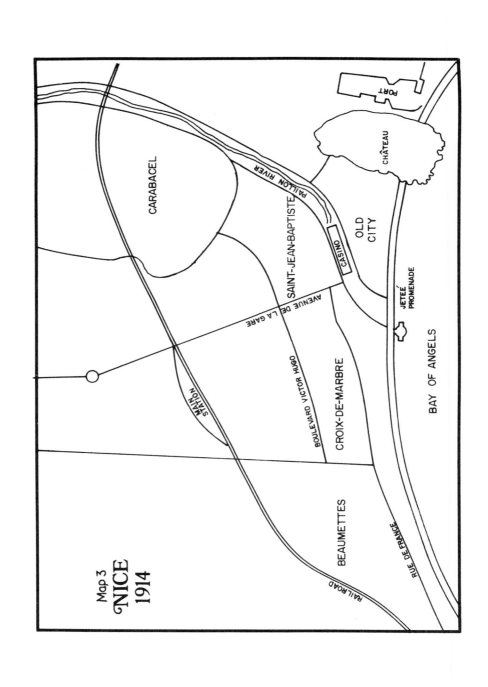

Map 3
NICE
1914

CARABACEL

MAIN STATION

BEAUMETTES

CROIX-DE-MARBRE

BOULEVARD VICTOR HUGO

AVENUE DE LA GARE

SAINT-JEAN-BAPTISTE

PAILLON RIVER

CASINO

OLD CITY

PORT

CHÂTEAU

RAILROAD

RUE DE FRANCE

JETÉE
PROMENADE

BAY OF ANGELS

concerned about the directions taken. Laissez-faire and *enrichissez-vous* ("get rich") formed the keynotes of both the imperial and republican administrations in Nice.

3

Luxury, Status, and the
Two Populations of Nice

BESIDES FOSTERING UNIQUE LAND-USE PATTERNS, Nice's tourist industry shaped the development of a distinctive urban population structure. Tourist cities, after all, have two separate populations: the transient tourists and the permanent local residents. Both populations evolve as their separate needs and desires change; yet, they are interdependent and continually interact with one another. These populations, like the resort cities themselves, seem to follow a definite maturation pattern, passing from one stage to another in a predictable progression. Taken together these changes in tastes, habits, and needs have an enormous impact on a resort city.

The first phase in the life of most tourist cities is that of aristocratic tourism. During this phase only a few people know of the pleasures a resort has to offer; and since communications with the resort are usually rudimentary, few are willing to make the expensive and complicated effort to visit the city. These fortunate few, however, are able to enjoy whatever advantages the area offers in a calm and unhurried manner. They usually make rather modest demands on their host city, at least during the first years following their "discovery."

The second stage in the development of a tourist city is that of worldly tourism; this usually comes only after a resort has acquired a reputation and a simplified means of access. This stage involves the arrival of large numbers of visitors who are mostly interested in entertainment and active self-enjoyment. The transition is painful and expensive for most tourist cities because it requires the development of elaborate and expensive infrastructures if the cities are to continue to attract worldly visitors.

The transformation of Nice from a center for *villégiature* to a resort for high-society people did not occur suddenly; it was the result of an evolutionary process that began sometime around 1875. Before then, most visitors came to Nice hoping that a winter spent in the warm sun and clean air would help cure whatever diseases ailed them. These "health egoists" wanted "to find rest, after the fatigue of a season in Paris or London, or to heal a constitution damaged by the rude climate of the North."[1] At least two-thirds of the winter residents came for reasons of health, and the rest, "who spent their winter toasting themselves like lizards," came largely because they sought repose.[2]

These "sick and shy" visitors who came to take the sun in Nice made rather light demands on the city. At the height of sun-and-air tourism in 1872 the *Phare du littoral,* Nice's leading newspaper, set forth a program that was supposed to insure the city's prosperity. To perfect itself for its winter guests, wrote the editors of the *Phare,* Nice had only to maintain the roads that the visitors used for walks and carriage excursions, spruce up the promenade des Anglais, reorganize the police force to insure perfect tranquility, keep down the dust, regulate the public carriage business, and eliminate public begging. Two years earlier, in 1870, the *Phare* had recommended the suppression of political agitation, a position presumably designed to encourage timid visitors who were fearful of Italian irredentism.[3] In 1875 the *Phare* published another program for improvement—similar in tone and in certain of its recommendations—that urged the city to focus on sanitary reform. This time the newspaper noted that Nice had nothing to fear from competing winter resort cities if it could only improve its water supply, expand the network of sewers, stop local washerwomen from washing laundry in the Paillon, illuminate the streets, and construct "inodorous free and pay" public toilets.[4]

Clearly, Nice's visitors during this period desired sun, air, peace, quiet, cleanliness, and rest. They had little interest in complex forms of entertainment, and neither the city nor private business made much of an attempt to provide them with entertainment facilities. Except for a sedate opera, Nice had virtually no public entertainment before the mid 1870s. "Our city," noted the spokesman for the committee charged with overseeing the municipal opera, "except for the sun and our agreeable promenades offers very little to retain the rich foreign colony. We possess neither monuments, nor museums, nor works of art to admire, [nor] hardly any clubs to attend." The question that occasioned this remark was whether or not the municipal council should give the opera a 28,000 franc subsidy for a dance company, a virtual necessity for any respectable nineteenth-century French opera house.[5]

Although the council approved the subsidy in 1872, the prefect, who had final authority over the municipal budget, later informed the city fathers that they could grant the subsidy only if they agreed to cut an equivalent amount from other budget items. Since the opera had already hired performers, the council had little choice but to continue the subsidy while making cuts elsewhere. Faced with this prefectorial intransigence, the council decided not to continue the subsidy after 1872, largely because they felt that the dance company was a luxury unappreciated by the city's visitors.[6]

The precarious financial condition of the opera and the shaky reception accorded the dance company suggest that Nice's winter residents were not particularly interested in sophisticated entertainment. *Hivernants* attended the opera, but efforts to make it competitive with Europe's finest failed because the visitors simply did not care to be actively entertained. The average visitor in this early phase of Nice's development preferred walks, carriage rides, and light, open-air concerts to the complicated and formalized fare available in the opera houses of Paris and Milan. As a *Phare du littoral* editorial entitled "Not Enough Music" pointed out, visitors came to Nice to enjoy the climate, not to be shut up indoors for concerts. Consequently, the editor argued, Nice had to provide more than the weekly ninety minutes of open-air music that was available in 1871. Moreover, the *Phare* continued, the music should be presented on days other than Sunday because many visitors were Protestant and kept the Sabbath, apparently even to the extent of avoiding open-air concerts.[7]

By the late 1870s the social events available in Nice during the winter season had become more oriented toward those who wished to see and be seen, to take an active part in leisure activities, and to consume complex and structured kinds of entertainment. The development of the carnival, Nice's most popular attraction during the late nineteenth and early twentieth centuries, is a case in point. The first carnival celebration took place in 1821 when the Sardinian court spent the winter in Nice. The carnival remained an annual event after that, but it was little more than an opportunity for local rowdies to carouse and let off steam; by 1848 it had degenerated into an annual brawl in which a winter visitor participated at his own peril. In 1863, shortly after Nice became French, the local chief of the national police force happily informed the minister of the interior that the carnival had passed that year without any serious incidents. It had been marked mainly by the violent throwing of confetti (a term which the agent used very loosely) that had caused considerable distress to persons not used to "these rather savage men." The throwing of flowers and pistachios (the traditional

The Carnival at Nice, c. 1860 (*courtesy of the Bibliothèque National, Paris*)

missiles) had almost ceased, he wrote; instead participants threw beans, chick peas, flour, and balls of soot. It seems highly unlikely that many tourists would have wanted to participate in such activities.[8]

In 1873, however, the city recognized that the carnival could help attract visitors to the city and established a festival committee to reorganize it. The committee directed its efforts toward making the carnival more attractive to visitors, moved it from the Old City to the New, and introduced events designed to integrate the tourist colony into the festivities. By lengthening the celebration and devising new activities that required large amounts of wealth and leisure, the committee took control of the carnival away from the permanent residents and gave it to the winter visitors. The committee's most important act was the creation in 1876 of the "Battle of Flowers" which rapidly became a showcase for elegance of all kinds. Essentially, the "battle" consisted of a parade of carriages elaborately decorated with flowers. The carriages drove up and down the promenade des Anglais giving the occupants an opportunity to toss bouquets at one another. The winter residents enthusiastically embraced this event and expended enormous amounts of time and energy in preparing themselves and their carriages for the battle. The festival committee, which always included some of the most distinguished members of the "foreign colony" (nonpermanent residents), also encouraged the construction of floats that were ever more extraordinary and costly. The carnival rapidly became the high point of the winter season and increasingly set the tone for it. The carnival's emphasis on elegance, luxury, and celebration helped to destroy the hegemony of the sun-and-air tourists and further emphasized the ascendency of those dedicated to enjoying themselves in a vigorous and ostentatious manner.[9]

The evolution of the prostitution industry in the late 1870s provides further evidence that the nature of Nice's visitors was changing. Although Nice had always had its share of prostitutes (*filles publiques*), they generally seemed to be permanent residents of the Old City with few ties to the foreign colony. After 1860 visitors usually avoided the Old City; and if the complete absence of complaints or observations of prostitution emanating from the usually prudish foreign colony is any indication, these women transacted little of their business with winter residents. Indeed, the only serious complaint in the prefectorial files of the 1860s concerns those women unfortunate enough to be locked up in the hospital with venereal disease. (In accordance with French customs of the time, Nice's municipal authorities carefully regulated the prostitutes and forced them to undergo periodic health examinations, sequestering those who were infected.)[10] The hospital was located in a rural area north of the city, and local peasants complained about visitors hoping to communicate with the women. According to a petition drafted by the peasants, these unwanted visitors

> audaciously enter the said yard or climb the walls . . . correspond with them by shouts and whistles to which they respond with other shouts, by the most obscene proposals, and revolting gestures. The farmer peasants of these fields are powerless to stop this commerce . . . [because] these often numerous rascals reply by threats.[11]

The only other complaints in the official files concerned army officers who brought prostitutes with them on a visit to Nice.

As in other French cities, the oldest profession flourished in Nice during the years after the annexation, but at a level much lower than one would expect, especially for a tourist city. Indeed, in 1866 a very sedate and straight-laced newspaper catering to the foreign colony even gloated about Nice's lack of prostitutes.

> Having no dandies, Nice has no kept women. Lyons, Marseilles and Bordeaux have theirs, as does Paris. . . . At the beginning of each winter season Lyons and Marseilles export to Nice some of their most brilliant subjects. These beautiful girls arrive and immediately arm themselves with fresh dresses [and] painted faces, nothing lacks. They have dreamed, these dear things, of Yankee dollars and Russian rubles, English pounds, and German florins. Alas! alas! In two days, after having made the tour of the city three or four times, paraded in the public garden and the promenade des Anglais . . . they return to their carriages . . . alone.[12]

The paper was clearly proud that these independent businesswomen had to move on to Monaco after having failed to find customers in Nice.

By 1873, however, prostitution had become more widespread in Nice, and the municipal council moved to reorganize and more carefully regulate the industry. Each prostitute had to purchase a health certificate and pay two and a half francs for each medical visit. The city also decided to levy a fee of three francs for the privilege of living in the municipal brothel (*la maison de tolérance*). This rent money would support a dispensary, defray the expenses of hospital treatment for women with venereal disease, and pay the salaries of two special health inspectors and of two special policemen.[13]

By 1876 it was clear that prostitution had become one of Nice's major growth industries. The *Chronique des stations hivernales* lamented the change: the Paillon was no longer the only plague affecting Nice, it complained; now the city had developed something that was "horrible and cancerous, the evil of the easy woman." The women were not permanent residents of Nice, but were instead followers of the "swallows of winter." Competition had become fierce, and the prostitutes moved from street to street instead of occupying just one section of the city. "Isn't it too much," wrote the *Chronique,* "that our theaters, our stylish restaurants, and our train cars are infested by 'the Tart'?" By 1883, one Parisian observer grumbled that these women were so plentiful that "each evening the arcades of the place Masséna became a branch of the sidewalks of the faubourg Montmartre." Indeed, it is quite probable that many winter tourists who lounged under those arcades would have been found a few years earlier in a Montmartre bar.[14]

Another indication that Nice's tourist population was no longer dominated by sun-and-air partisans was the development of Nice's gambling industry. The first effort to establish a casino in Nice had failed in 1872 when a privately operated house, the Casino International, went bankrupt—largely, one suspects, because *hivernants* did not sufficiently patronize its gambling tables or its café and restaurant. The owner, a composer named Leopold Amat, sold his failing business to a private club, le Cercle de la Méditerranée.[15] Nevertheless, municipal leaders felt that a casino was essential if the tourist industry were to prosper; and therefore, they proposed building a city-owned casino. In order to avoid purchasing prime building land, these enthusiasts proposed constructing the municipal casino on a platform erected over the bed of the Paillon River.

Although a number of entrepreneurs had wanted to use the Paillon for building space, the first plan to receive any kind of official approval was submitted in 1875. The proposal, submitted by the Marquis d'Espony de Saint Paul, involved building a huge "crystal palace" that would include not only a casino but a covered garden, galleries in which to hang paintings, a library, reading rooms, exhibition rooms, a café, a restaurant, a billiard room, and a large theater. "At last," said Espony, "all the distractions that the foreign colony could desire will be at its disposition." The scale of Espony's project was massive: the casino and the accompanying gardens alone were to cover some 10,000 square meters. The entrepreneur wanted no subsidy, however, only a ninety-year concession, with the casino reverting to the city thereafter. The committee charged with studying the proposal approved it, noting that the casino would "create a meeting place in bad weather [and was] destined to give the foreign colony especially all the advantages and comfort it is accustomed to finding in winter spas."[16]

This preliminary approval was followed by a public meeting designed to gauge the strength of public support for the project. After a spirited discussion, those in attendance urged rejection of the scheme—largely because it would obstruct the panoramic view of the Mediterranean from the banks of the Paillon and because owners of river-front real estate feared the casino would depress property values. They threatened to demand high indemnities from the city if construction proceeded. Faced with this vocal opposition, the committee reversed itself and recommended dropping the project. Nice's future, it agreed, was inextricably tied to sun-and-air tourism, and no building should go up where "one enjoys the most beautiful view a city can offer by the presence of the sea, free from all obstruction."[17]

Yet the idea of constructing a casino over the Paillon would not die. The controversy surrounding Espony de Saint Paul's application clearly showed that opinion in Nice was divided over the question of the casino and that a change of municipal administrations or of tourists' expectations might tip the balance in favor of a future builder. Between 1876 and 1878 both of these changes did indeed take place.

The first development that made covering the Paillon politically feasible was the January 1878 election of Alfred Borriglione as mayor of Nice. Borriglione, an ambitious man, hoped to bring Nice into the front rank of great European cities by embarking on a massive program of public works; the casino was to be the cornerstone. Borriglione was the first man to lead Nice who understood (or thought he understood) the enormous energy and creativity that could be liberated when one combined capital, technology, and initiative. He believed that front-rank status for Nice could be attained quickly if only sufficient effort were expended; he viewed opponents of his plans as afflicted with Mediterranean sloth. Not surprisingly, those conservatives who had torpedoed Espony's "crystal palace" found themselves totally ignored by the new municipal administration.[18]

Borriglione's plans were furthered by a coincidental shift in the tourist population. The rapidly growing portion of Nice's visitors who came primarily in search of entertainment demanded much more than peace, quiet, and sunshine. To keep their interest in the city alive, Nice had to provide sophisticated entertainment facilities rivaling those in the European capitals, where race tracks, gambling houses, and dance halls were abundant. These new winter visitors found the sun and air in Nice pleasant, but the climate was not enough to bring them back year after year.

By 1879 the municipal council had definitely made up its mind to encourage a new plan to construct a casino over the Paillon. Omar Lazard, the successful entrepreneur, proposed building the casino several hundred meters inland from the sea in order to appease the sun-and-air visitors who opposed having their panoramic view of the sea blocked.[19]

By giving Lazard the concession for the Casino Municipal, then,

Nice's city fathers believed that they were satisfying both factions of the tourist population. The sun-and-air group would be pleased because the unpleasant odors of the Paillon's stagnant bed would decrease and because they could continue to enjoy their cherished view of the sea. The growing group of action-oriented tourists (*mondains,* or "worldly visitors"), on the other hand, would finally have a casino where they could gamble and where their wives and children could be more or less constantly entertained. Borriglione and his supporters reasoned that even the inhabitants of the Old City would benefit because the large platform over the Paillon would bind their quarters to the new city. The only losers would be the washerwomen who would find their operating space along the banks greatly decreased. "It is certain, gentlemen," a member of the special study commission remarked, "if the city of Nice can realize the project of having a casino, a center of attraction in the middle of the city, and at almost no cost cover a large part of the Paillon, she will have realized a beautiful dream."[20]

Besides the casino, a number of other commercial enterprises directed toward entertainment-minded tourists were started in Nice during the late 1870s. One such establishment was the Jetée-Promenade, an elabo-

Interior of the Casino Municipal (*courtesy of the Bibliothèque National, Paris*)

rate casino built on pilings that had been driven into the ocean bed several yards from the beach. Begun in 1880 and modeled after a similar casino in Brighton, the Jetée was built by a British firm and was constructed under rather confusing circumstances. First, Nice's contract with the builders of the Casino Municipal forbade city fathers from authorizing any other casino in the city; and second, the promoters never asked the city for authorization to build. Instead, apparently, they received permission from French national authorities who controlled the seabed. The British promoters did, however, ask the City of Nice to allow construction of a walkway from the beach to the casino. The city fathers, fulfilling the letter of their contract with Lazard, approved on the condition that the Jetée was not to be considered a casino! Ultimately, the owners of the Jetée persuaded the prefect to overrule Nice's municipal council and give them the necessary authorization. The Jetée was a splendid monument to Victorian cast-iron and glass construction, built with the wealthiest of Nice's *mondains* in mind.

Besides construction of the municipal casino and the Jetée, other less visible innovations were taking place that reflected the transformation

The Jetée Promenade *(courtesy of the Musée Masséna, Nice)*

of Nice's tourist population. In 1875, the city administration began efforts to establish a pigeon shoot on the hill where ruins of the old castle stood. The following year, members of the foreign colony built a roller-skating rink where "novices in the art of skating" could practice. These changes pointed to the arrival of a new breed of tourist, no longer satisfied with sun and air.[21]

The most striking proof of this transformation can be found in the city's budget for public holidays. Between 1875 and 1910 the amount budgeted for festivals increased dramatically (see graph 3). To be sure, Nice was growing rapidly, but the increase in such expenditures was

GRAPH 3

Expenditures Budgeted for Public Festivals, 1861–1910

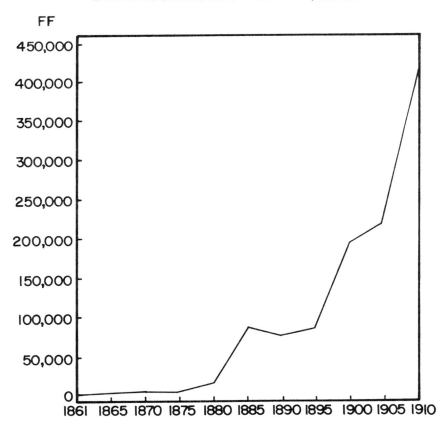

Source: Budgets of the city of Nice, 1861–1910.

clearly all out of proportion to any growth in either its permanent or floating populations. When one compares these monies to those budgeted for street cleaning (a service that is closely tied to the physical development of a city), it becomes clear that Nice's leaders were responding to qualitative, rather than quantitative, changes in the population. Between 1875 and 1910 the amount spent on street cleaning grew from 27,000 to 281,000 francs, a ten-fold increase. At the same time the amount budgeted for festivals and public holidays increased from 5,000 to 414,000 francs. By 1910 Nice was supporting a variety of activities ranging from its traditional carnival to rowing regattas. With the exception of a modest subsidy for the Bastille Day celebration, all this spending was designed to attract and entertain action-oriented winter visitors.[22]

The transformation of the tourist population also changed Nice's construction industry. Before the *mondain* period, most tourists preferred to live in villas that housed, usually, a single family and its servants. In keeping with their desire for peace, quiet, sun, and air, most of these visitors built their villas in the countryside, away from the city, surrounded by ornamental gardens of flowering trees and shrubs. Although some of the villas were magnificent, most were relatively modest country cottages. The changeover from sun-and-air to *mondain* tourism brought with it a demand for different accommodations. The entertainment-oriented tourists, although at least as desirous of luxury as their more sedate brethren, cared little for bucolic pleasures, preferring instead to see and be seen and to live amid color and light; for them, country villas were boring and not desirable. Their residences had to be luxurious, of course, and had to liberate inhabitants from all domestic cares that might interfere with more worldly pursuits. Above all, their quarters had to offer opportunities for the display of wealth, leisure, and magnificence. In short, the *mondain* tourists insisted on the right to consume conspicuously, and their residences provided a main outlet for this intention.[23]

As usual, builders hurried to meet the demand: the type of accommodation that emerged was the grand hotel. To be sure, Nice had had a number of hotels during the development of sun-and-air tourism, but they tended to resemble modern-day pensions, being rather modest places often located in residential neighborhoods.[24] The grand hotels were different. Typified by the magnificent Hôtel Ruhl, which was built in 1884, these establishments offered the ultimate in luxury and opulence. Equipped with ostentatious facades (the Ruhl's minarets became world-famous), luxurious dining rooms and lobbies, and enormous staffs of servants of all descriptions, these hotels satisfied the newer tourists' need for conspicuous consumption as a quiet country villa never could. The years

58

The Hotel Regina *(courtesy of the Musée Masséna, Nice)*

following the completion of the Ruhl saw the rapid construction of many similar hotels, particularly in the quarter of Cimiez, which became fashionable and accessible after 1881. Hotels bearing names such as the Grand Hôtel, the Riviera Palace, or the Winter Palace provided the most fashionable winter homes for visitors to Nice. At least one local historian has noted with astonishment how precipitously villa construction declined after 1881.[25]

Who were these *mondains* who had taken control of the fortunes of Nice from the "sick and timid"? It goes without saying that they were wealthy—practically all of the new, *mondain* visitors had either inherited or acquired fortunes and were willing to spend lavishly for goods, services, and entertainment in Nice. They came from the ruling, business, or financial classes and from the highest levels of polite society. During *la belle époque,* Nice provided members of the European and American leisure classes with every imaginable way to spend their money and their time. For the men, the days were filled by trips to clubs, casinos, cafés, and restaurants. The women engaged in endless rounds of formal visits

59

or, in turn, received visitors "at home." They spent an enormous amount of time selecting, purchasing, arranging, and changing their clothes and jewelry; preparing for balls and parties; and planning for the festivities that surrounded the carnival. In general, these society lives were predictable and dull, and although great sums of money changed hands in Nice during these years, it was a rare winter resident who did or said anything that would be remembered after the end of any particular season.[26]

The changes just described in the composition of Nice's tourist population occurred so gradually as to be practically invisible to many people. Yet by the early 1880s, it had become apparent to all that the tourist colony had evolved dramatically since the 1860s. Disagreement existed, however, as to whether these changes were for the better; good arguments could be made by both sides. Proponents of the idea that Nice should remain a haven for Europe's sick and tired argued that the sun-and-air tourists were peaceful, unobtrusive, and asked only that the city provide quality municipal services and a reasonable level of security. Furthermore, these visitors tended to be stable guests: many had committed themselves to the city by purchasing villas and returning to Nice year after year. Supporters of the idea that Nice should become the focal point for fashionable society (*la vie mondaine*), on the other hand, argued that if Nice were ever to maximize its full economic potential, it would have to be much more than a sanitarium by the sea. If the wheels of Nice's commercial machine were to turn faster, they would have to be lubricated by large amounts of free-flowing money. Although the sun-and-air visitors were wealthy, they did not spend heavily for goods or services beyond housing and food. The *mondain* visitors, on the other hand, were conspicuous consumers, willing to spend extravagantly for all kinds of goods and services. However, the newer tourists did not seem to be willing to make a commitment to the city, preferring instead to leave their choice of winter residence open from year to year. Their unpredictable behavior, their fickle tastes, and their love of gambling and carousing made many Niçois fearful for the future of their city. Furthermore, without the lures of tradition or property ownership, the new visitors tended to be skittish when confronted by unfavorable rumors or events in the financial world. In spite of these apprehensions, Nice's future pattern had been determined: its days as the sanatarium of Europe were over. For better or for worse, the future would revolve around the most sophisticated and demanding members of *la belle époque*'s monied classes.

The influx of these sophisticated visitors necessarily had a profound impact on Nice's resident population, and its evolution paralleled that of

The Promenade des Anglais, c. 1900 (courtesy of the Bibliothèque National, Paris)

the tourist population. The new demands of the *mondain* tourists meant the development of whole new industries that employed thousands. Because of this dynamism, the city grew during the last half of the nineteenth century from a small town of only regional importance to a metropolis; and by 1911 Nice's permanent population had swollen to almost 143,000. Professionals and workers from all over Europe flocked to Nice, and although many were transient, most seemed willing to tie their fortunes to the tourist industry and become permanent residents of the Riviera. To study Nice's people, then, is to examine a population whose size, composition, and distribution was shaped by tourism.

One of the most important effects of the city's dependence on tourism was the tendency of the population to become highly stratified: between 1872 and 1911, Nice's population became segregated by social, occupational, and ethnic groupings. The diverse neighborhoods, with all income groups living in close proximity, that had previously marked the city disappeared rapidly under the influence of tourism. The tourist quarters acted like magnets, drawing the wealthiest citizens of Nice to them. At the same time the Old City which historically had had a diverse population became a lower-class ghetto, shunned both by tourists and by Nice's most prosperous permanent citizens.

As discussed in chapter 1, soon after the arrival of the first English *hivernants* in the eighteenth century, it became clear that most tourists preferred residences away from the central city. Most winter visitors made their homes on the undeveloped right bank of the Paillon River, and the two new quarters of Croix-de-Marbre and St.-Jean-Baptiste were dotted with their villas. The permanent residents, on the other hand, lived in the Old City (Vieille Ville). By 1872 Nice had practically become two cities. On the right bank of the Paillon was the tourist colony—Croix-de-Marbre and St.-Jean-Baptiste—deserted during the summer but occupied by some of Europe's wealthiest people in the winter. On the left bank stood the Old City, home to a majority of Nice's permanent residents. These three neighborhoods changed dramatically between 1872 and 1911; and by World War I, together they formed the central city, occupied by permanent residents who varied greatly in occupational and social status.

An appropriate place to begin comparing the Old City, Croix-de-Marbre, and St.-Jean-Baptiste is to study the residential distribution of the heads-of-household who occupied the lowest rungs of the employment ladder. In the context of the French censuses, this category is best defined as that of *journalier,* or day laborer. For the purposes of this analysis, to the *journaliers* have been added those whose job-titles implied occasional labor.[27] By examining the residential patterns of these people, it is possible to obtain a preliminary view of the social composition of the three neighborhoods under consideration.

Between 1872 and 1911, the percentage of the Old City's population employed as day laborers jumped from 15 percent to 24 percent (see computergraphic images 1–3).[28] At the same time, the percentage of laborers in the two other neighborhoods remained extremely low: in Croix-de-Marbre, it varied from 3 to 6 percent (see images 4–6); in St.-Jean-Baptiste, it stayed at 4 percent (see images 7–9). For Nice as a whole, the figure varied little, from 11 to 13 percent. In addition, the number of *journaliers* per block (1000 square meters) showed the same pattern: in the Old City, the density increased from 33 per block in 1872 to 49 in 1911; in Croix-de-Marbre and St.-Jean-Baptiste, the figure varied between 2 and 4 per block. In the entire city the average number of *journaliers* per block declined slightly, from 10 in 1872 to 8 in 1911. It is clear, therefore, that as the city grew, workers employed in these menial occupations tended to congregate in the city center.

Although these differences are striking, they do not necessarily prove that Nice was becoming occupationally stratified. After all, workers at the bottom of the occupational ladder often are forced to live in the oldest (and cheapest) housing a city has to offer. It is useful, therefore, to look at a higher occupational grouping, that of skilled construction workers.[29] If their proportion increased in the Old City, one could argue that it was becoming the home of more workers, not merely more unskilled workers. On the other hand, if the proportion of skilled laborers decreased, it would be evidence that they were abandoning the Old City for other neighborhoods. Although neither conclusion is demonstrated dramatically, the weight of the evidence suggests a departure of skilled workers from the Old City and their redistribution throughout the city at large. Between 1872 and 1911 the percentage of construction workers in the Old City declined slightly from 16 percent to 14 percent. At the same time, the proportion of skilled construction workers in the two tourist quarters declined even more: in Croix-de-Marbre, it fell from 8 percent in 1872 to 5 percent in 1911, and in St.-Jean-Baptiste, it dropped from 18 to 6 percent. The proportion for Nice as a whole fell from 13 to 11 percent, the same rate as for the Old City. Skilled construction workers, then, tended to distribute themselves evenly throughout the city, with the exception of the main tourist quarters. Day laborers remained the dominant occupational group in the Old City, and they plus the construction workers accounted for 42 percent of the employed population in 1911.

But what of the other side of the coin, the distribution of inhabitants employed in the highest professional and commercial occupations?[30]

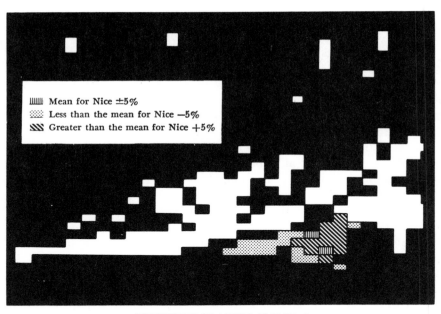

COMPUTERGRAPHIC IMAGE 1

DAY LABORERS, OLD CITY, 1872

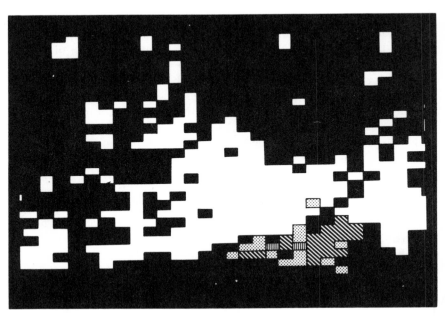

COMPUTERGRAPHIC IMAGE 2

DAY LABORERS, OLD CITY, 1891

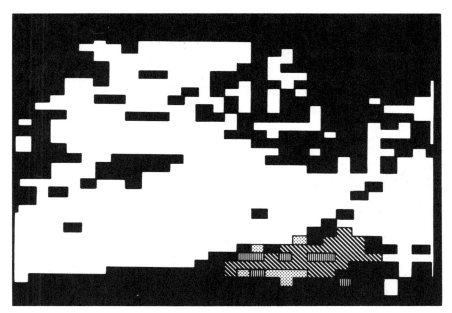

COMPUTERGRAPHIC IMAGE 3

DAY LABORERS, OLD CITY, 1911

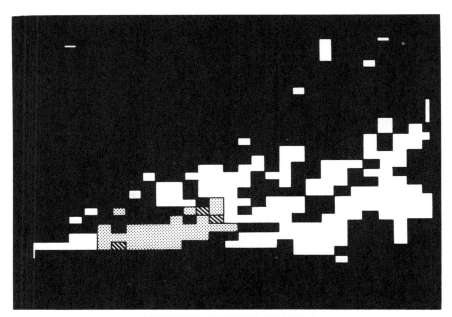

COMPUTERGRAPHIC IMAGE 4

DAY LABORERS, CROIX-DE-MARBRE, 1872

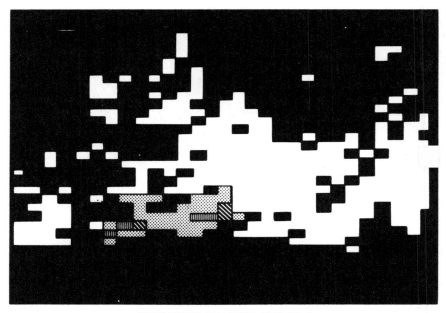

COMPUTERGRAPHIC IMAGE 5

DAY LABORERS, CROIX-DE-MARBRE, 1891

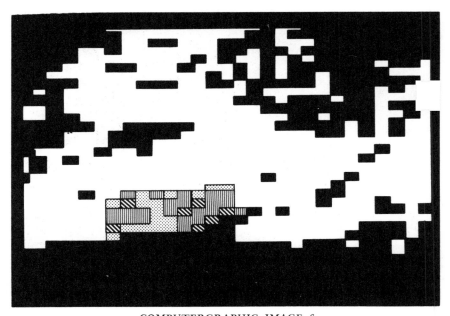

COMPUTERGRAPHIC IMAGE 6

DAY LABORERS, CROIX-DE-MARBRE, 1911

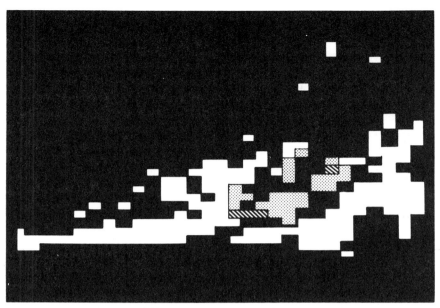

COMPUTERGRAPHIC IMAGE 7

Day Laborers, St.-Jean-Baptiste, 1872

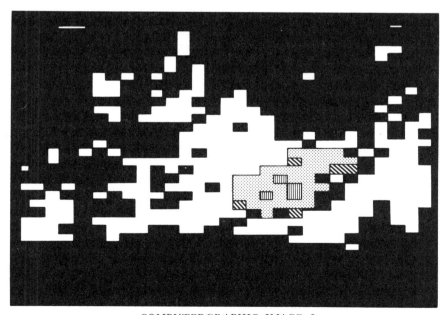

COMPUTERGRAPHIC IMAGE 8

Day Laborers, St.-Jean-Baptiste, 1891

67

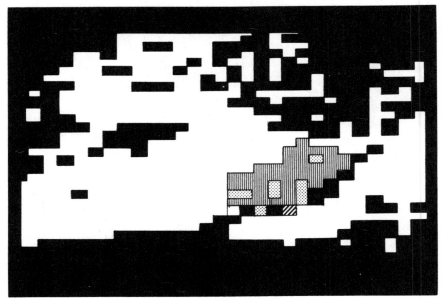

COMPUTERGRAPHIC IMAGE 9
DAY LABORERS, ST.-JEAN-BAPTISTE, 1911

When the distribution of these groups is examined, the pattern of occupational stratification becomes clear. Between 1872 and 1911 the proportion of professionals in the Old City decreased from 14 percent in 1872 to 6 percent in 1911. Concurrently, the tourist quarters attracted more and more of these upper-income people, causing their proportion to vary between 19 and 24 percent in Croix-de-Marbre and from 20 to 26 percent in St.-Jean-Baptiste. At the same time the proportion of professionals in the city as a whole declined from 14 percent in 1872 to 11 percent in 1911. By 1911 the Old City contained so few members of the upper-income group that they would have been practically invisible when compared to the *journaliers.*

As the preceding analysis indicates, a considerable amount of occupational stratification took place between 1872 and 1911. The Old City, the traditional home of Nice's business and professional classes, was transformed from an occupationally and socially diverse neighborhood into a lower-class ghetto dominated by laborers. And, in a parallel development, the quarters influenced by tourists rapidly became the preferred place of residence for Nice's upper classes.

As the populations of the Old City, Croix-de-Marbre, and St.-Jean-

Baptiste were becoming stratified occupationally, a similar sorting process caused the same areas to become identifiable according to national origin of their residents. Essentially, this meant that while the Old City was losing its occupational diversity, it was acquiring an ethnic character distinct from the other neighborhoods. Thus, while the rest of Nice was becoming more cosmopolitan because of the success of the tourist industry, the Old City was losing the cosmopolitan character it once had and was becoming dominated by Italian immigrants.

The fact that Nice was home for thousands of Italians is not surprising. After all, those born in Nice before 1860 were Italian nationals and became French only when they chose to renounce their Italian identification.[31] Furthermore, most native Niçois spoke Niçard, a language related to Provençal, but one that contained many Italian elements. Thus, the city was a logical place for penniless, unemployed Italians to live. They could find work in one of Nice's dynamic tourist-related industries and at the same time be near their homeland, only thirty miles away. And they came to Nice in increasing numbers throughout the nineteenth century.

Although all areas of the city contained large numbers of Italians, in the Old City, Croix-de-Marbre, and St.-Jean-Baptiste the proportions deviated significantly from the city's overall average. Table 3 indicates

TABLE 3

Nationality of Neighborhood Populations, 1872–1911

(By Percentages)

	1872	1891	1911
French			
Croix-de-Marbre	76	73	71
St.-Jean-Baptiste	91	75	78
Old City	77	67	63
Nice	81	69	66
Italian			
Croix-de-Marbre	19	15	17
St.-Jean-Baptiste	7	15	16
Old City	22	26	33
Nice	16	22	29
French and Italian			
Croix-de-Marbre	95	88	88
St.-Jean-Baptiste	98	90	94
Old City	99	93	96
Nice	97	91	95

that during the latter part of the nineteenth century, the Old City was becoming the home of an ever-larger proportion of Nice's Italian population, while the size of the Italian populations in the newer tourist neighborhoods remained fairly stable. In only one period was the percent of Italians in the two right-bank suburbs above the mean for the city as a whole; and only once did the Italian population of either of these areas climb. This increase, which occurred in St.-Jean-Baptiste, was probably a consequence of the neighborhood's newness in 1872. So as the Old City was becoming packed with people employed in menial occupations, it was also becoming filled with Italian immigrants. By 1911, one-third of its population was of Italian origin. The newer quarters, on the other hand, seem to have had an Italian population that stabilized at about 16 percent. Nice's overall average climbed from 16 percent in 1872 to 29 percent in 1911.

An analysis of the rest of Nice's population indicates one clear characteristic: nearly all of the non-Italians were Frenchmen. The proportion of Frenchmen living in the Old City, Croix-de-Marbre, and St.-Jean-Baptiste varied from 63 percent to 91 percent (see table 3). During this period the Old City always had a smaller proportion of French nationals than either of the other two neighborhoods or than the city as a whole. When the percentages of French nationals and of Italians are added together, one finds that Nice's permanent population was composed solely of these two groups. The absence of significant numbers of foreigners (other than Italians) is not too surprising. After all, few *hivernants* lived permanently in Nice, and the censuses were taken in late March or early April. Thus, under the best of circumstances, the census reflected only those foreigners who were permanently installed in Nice. Also, although the census-takers were supposed to enumerate all of the people they encountered who were not associated with various officially defined organizations, it appears that the enumerators were reluctant to include visitors who were only temporary residents.[32]

It is interesting to note that the French-born population tended to distribute itself geographically in Nice's neighborhoods according to birthplace. The Old City, which was the main residence of Nice's Italians, was also home to a large percentage of Niçois (see table 4).

When the French-born population of the tourist quarters is examined, one finds relatively high proportions of immigrants from other parts of rural France. It is not surprising that this great difference between the Old City and the tourist quarters existed in 1872. After all, neither Croix-de-Marbre nor St.-Jean-Baptiste had been part of Nice for long, and people born in those areas would have been correct in reporting to the census-takers that they had not been born in the city. It is unlikely, however, that this was the explanation in later years. Shunned by immigrants, the Old City seemed to be viewed as a kind of haven by native-born Niçois, desirous of avoiding life in the tourist-dominated quarters.

TABLE 4

BIRTHPLACE OF NEIGHBORHOOD FRENCH POPULATIONS, 1872–1911

(BY PERCENTAGES)

	1872	1891	1911
Nice			
Croix-de-Marbre	44	....	28
St.-Jean-Baptiste	46	....	32
Old City	60	....	42
Nice	56	....	32
Rural France*			
Croix-de-Marbre	29	....	36
St.-Jean-Baptiste	43	....	40
Old City	15	....	19
Nice	24	....	30

* Includes all parts of France except Nice proper and the major cities (Paris, Lyons, Marseilles, Bordeaux, Lille, and Toulouse).

Thus, it seems clear that more than the gravelly banks of the Paillon separated the Old City from the tourist quarters of the right bank. In the course of the nineteenth century, the Old City became a city unto itself, an area that had little in common with the new quarters of Nice. The distance between the Old City and the newer quarters was not merely physical; it was marked by differences in occupation, origin, language, and culture. Today, it is difficult for a visitor even to find the Old City; it is skillfully hidden by an almost impenetrable palisade of building fronts. This may seem peculiar to a tourist interested in discovering the quaint, but it is more understandable in light of Nice's development during the nineteenth century. By World War I, the Old City had become a kind of ghetto whose typical resident was a native Niçois or Italian who spoke Niçard or Italian and who worked as a day laborer somewhere in Nice. The Old City had lost its earlier cosmopolitan character; its social and cultural dynamism had moved beyond the Paillon, and with its passing went the hopes of those who wanted to view the Old City as the heart and mind of Nice.

One can only speculate as to why Nice developed such a stratified social configuration. Certainly the relatively high living expenses on the right bank tended to drive away the very poor, while the newer buildings attracted the rich. Also, the cosmopolitan values and culture of the wealthy tourists probably attracted members of Nice's upwardly mobile classes who wished to learn from them, to associate with them, perhaps to join them. A final explanation, however, seems more persuasive. By 1880, Nice had become a city led by men whose overriding concern was to satisfy the desires of the tourists. These leaders knew that without tourists Nice would be only another small, Mediterranean town. To prevent this regression, they allocated municipal resources and provided services in such a way as to please the tourists and to persuade them to return to Nice again and again. Thus, the tourist quarters received the best the city could offer. Throughout the last half of the nineteenth century, these neighborhoods had water, drainage, and sanitation services far superior to those in the Old City and, indeed, in most other European cities. The Niçois who could leave the Old City did so, secure in the knowledge that life in the tourist quarters would be much pleasanter. Living on the right bank would ensure them an equal share of municipal attention, at least while the tourists were present.

4

Tourism and the Urban Economy

URBAN TRANSITION IS SELDOM PAINLESS, and Nice's efforts to adapt to a changing population structure and to its new worldly visitors would have caused considerable institutional instability under the best of conditions. The last quarter of the nineteenth century, however, was marked by the near collapse of the French financial system and an accompanying depression. Depending as the city did on luxury expenditures, Nice was hard hit and suffered through years of bankruptcies, depressed land values, and severe economic readjustment. During these trying years nearly every institution that local leaders thought would guarantee Nice's future prosperity was damaged or destroyed. This institutional breakdown, coupled with the effects of the financial crisis, transformed the city's relationship to its visitors and clarified its place in the larger French society. The period illustrated, as nothing else could, the fragility of a tourist economy.

As noted above, the postannexation years were prosperous ones for Nice and its citizens. The growing influx of tourists provided builders, hotel owners, and other purveyors of goods and services with a constantly expanding source of income; prosperity seemed assured, at least for the foreseeable future. Speculation in land and buildings proceeded apace between 1878 and 1882, allowing the construction industry to support thousands of workers.[1] Taxes collected on land sales more than doubled between 1877 and 1881, rising from 2,039,206 francs to 5,285,275 francs. This feverish activity promoted consumption: between 1877 and 1880, the federal agency responsible for collecting indirect taxes reported a 15 percent increase in wine consumption, a 40 percent increase in liquor sales, and a 60 percent increase in the consumption of tobacco. The number of rail passengers who stopped off in Nice increased, growing from 701,885 travelers in 1877 to 1,214,716 in 1881—up 73 percent. Builders erected some 1,250 new buildings between 1876 and 1881 and between 1879 and 1881 constructed 274 apartment buildings, averaging four stories each. As Mayor Borriglione noted, Nice's growth from 1877 to 1882 had been so astonishing "that today it has asserted itself in an irresistible way." Like most members of Nice's business community, Borriglione and his administration believed that the city's economic achievements since annexation would continue unabated in future years. A phrase popular at the time typified the confidence of Nice's leaders: "It must be done, done again, and done quickly."[2]

Mayor Borriglione's confidence was based on the widely shared assumption that the prosperity of the late '70s and early '80s resulted from powerful developments that could not be halted except by a disaster such as a major war. Barring this, most Niçois agreed, visitors would flock to Nice in growing numbers; more buildings would be constructed; more money would be spent in the city; and more municipal revenues could be generated and expended in perfecting municipal services. In short, the spiral of prosperity would become ever wider and move ever faster until one day Nice could truly rank itself as one of the capitals of Europe.

Although enthusiasts such as Borriglione correctly predicted Nice's long-term future in general outlines, they underestimated the likelihood of a short-term catastrophe. The city's prosperity during the late 1870s and early 1880s was part of a national financial "bubble" and reflected a wave of speculative activity throughout France. Between 1878 and 1882, investment in stocks and instruments of credit overwhelmed parts of the French economy. New corporations were formed at an alarming rate, and the sales of their stock, combined with the millions of new offerings made by established firms, provided more than sufficient food for the speculative appetite. During the first four months of 1879, for example, 350 million francs worth of new issues were offered on the Paris stock exchange. By the first quarter of 1880 this figure had almost quintupled to 1.7 billion francs; and during the year 1879–1880 the total value of offerings rose to 4 billion francs. In 1881, 430 new corporations were created in Paris alone, with a total capital of almost 2 billion francs; and in addition, a number of new banks were founded.[3] The speculative bubble engulfed France's entire financial structure. As the *Revue des deux mondes* worried in 1881, "All of France's financial forces together are not enough to absorb the securities that have been created during the last few years, and the production of [them] unfortunately does not seem to be slowing down." Indeed, the investment level of 1882 was not reached again until 1908.[4]

One of the firms most severely affected by these speculative pressures was the Lyons bank, L'Union Générale. Founded in 1878 by a vigorous entrepreneur, Eugène Bontoux, the Union Générale prospered in the feverish financial climate of France's second city, and the buying and selling of its stock became a main occupation for Lyonnais from all professions and occupations. The bank stock became so popular between March and December 1881 that its value increased from 1,250 francs to 2,815 francs per share, a rise of 125 percent. Speculation in the stock of the Union Générale proceeded in a manner common to other financial bubbles. Beginning with the day that investors began purchasing stock on the assumption that it could be resold at a gain in the near future (regardless of its ability to produce regular income), speculation progressed with buyers purchasing stock at any price on the assumption that they could make a profit on it later the same day. Also, as the fever mounted, more and more people from progressively lower economic categories became involved. The enormous profits that had been realized throughout 1881 persuaded landowners and investors alike that their savings could be put to best use by buying bank paper.[5]

Unfortunately for purchasers of Union Générale stock (as well as for buyers of other banking stocks), prices could go down as rapidly as they had gone up, and beginning in the first week in January 1882, they did just that. Stock of the Banque de Lyon et de la Loire, another popular issue, fell from a high of 1,400 francs per share on January 1 to 1,040 on January 4 to 540 on January 30. For a time, the Union Générale resisted the collapse in values by employing the time-honored ruse of repurchasing its own stock, but by mid January it could no longer resist the wave of sellers. Between 16 January and 19 January 1882, Union Générale stock lost over 50 percent of its value, falling from 2,800 francs to 1,300 francs. During only one day, January 19, the stock lost 1,200 francs per share. Although Bontoux made heroic efforts to save himself and his bank, he failed, and on January 30 the Union Générale suspended payments. Bontoux was jailed and later sentenced to five years in prison for his financial dealings.[6]

The collapse of the Union Générale had an effect on France far out of proportion to the economic losses it caused. The fall of the Union Générale did not, of course, cause the depression of the 1880s, but like the American stock market crash of 1929, its collapse was symptomatic of grave underlying disorder, and it signaled that the prosperity of the early years of the Third Republic was over. As the symptoms of financial panic radiated out from the exchanges of Paris, Lyons, and Marseilles, banking activity declined, investment slowed precipitously, and, ultimately, general commerce slowed almost to a halt. Too much of the nation's capital had been invested in unproductive speculative enterprises; too little had been employed in creating useful goods and services; and France's banking structure was too inflexible to remedy the situation without the aid of a general depression (see table 5). As the economist Léon Say has pointed out, "If speculation had not been led

TABLE 5

FRENCH WHOLESALE PRICE INDEX, 1860–1914

Year	Index*	Year	Index
1860	144	1888	96
1861	142	1889	100
1862	142	1890	100
1863	143	1891	98
1864	141	1892	95
1865	132	1893	94
1866	134	1894	87
1867	131	1895	85
1868	132	1896	82
1869	130	1897	83
1870	133	1898	86
1871	138	1899	93
1872	144	1900	99
1873	144	1901	95
1874	132	1902	94
1875	129	1903	96
1876	130	1904	94
1877	131	1905	98
1878	120	1906	104
1879	117	1907	109
1880	120	1908	101
1881	117	1909	101
1882	114	1910	108
1883	110	1911	113
1884	101	1912	118
1885	99	1913	116
1886	95	1914	118
1887	92		

* 1901–1910 = 100.
Source: Annuaire statistique de la France 47 (1931):393*–94*.

astray into this path [bank paper] it would have been led astray into another. . . . The country was brought to a standstill in order to liquidate the enormous losses that it had experienced."[7]

Although the economic crisis affected all parts of France, it struck Nice later and more sharply than other French cities where growth had been less precipitous and where prosperity rested on a firmer foundation than tourism. Nice's economy had enough momentum to prevent the depression from affecting the city immediately. The city's economy was not hard hit until 1883. The course of the crisis is clearly visible in the curve of the receipts of the *octroi*, the municipal excise tax levied on commodities brought into the city. These receipts grew steadily through 1882, even though wholesale prices were falling. In 1883, however, growth abruptly ceased, and the value of most commodities brought into the city declined significantly. Graph 4, which gives comparative levels

GRAPH 4

RECEIPTS OF THE MUNICIPAL EXCISE TAX, 1876–1885

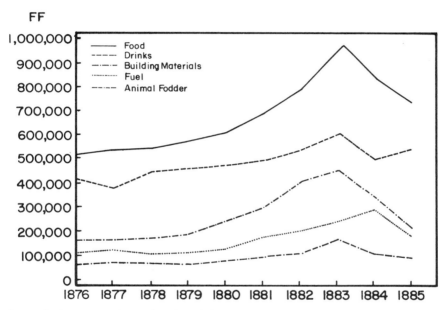

Source: Budgets of the city of Nice, 1876–1885.

of the receipts for several commodities, indicates the course of Nice's prosperity in the late 1870s and early 1880s. The abrupt change in the value of building materials imported into Nice is particularly important because it directly indicates the activity of Nice's second major industry, construction. Indeed, for many permanent residents of Nice, and especially for those of the Old City, construction was all important: it was their only available occupation. Both the predepression 1872 census and the postdepression 1891 census indicated that 40 percent of all employed persons in the Old City were laborers.[8]

While previously planned construction kept the hammers pounding through 1883, those individuals and businesses directly involved in serving the tourist population felt the impact of the crisis most immediately. Although the collapse in the value of financial paper did not occur until near the middle of the 1882–83 season, the general instability of the money markets during the late fall caused many to forego a winter in Nice. The 1882–83 season, while not disastrous, was much worse than any previous season since 1870–71. The *hivernants* who did come to Nice arrived late in the season, and those in the business of providing goods and services to the tourists watched with dismay as villas stood unrented and expensive trinkets tarnished in the shops. *La Colonie étrangère,* a newspaper published for the winter residents, noted that Nice had simply become too expensive for many visitors. More and more of them could no longer afford "the excessive prices that have been asked in recent years for a Niçois welcome." The newspaper advised that before the businessmen inflated their prices, they should remember an old local proverb, "No money, no Nice."[9]

Although France's general economic decline was the major cause of Nice's misfortunes, local businessmen seemed unable or unwilling to see that Nice's economy had become dependent on events in Paris and Lyons, over which they had no control. Long accustomed to a slower and more independent pace, the people of Nice had never before faced one of the basic truths of modern economic life: that all segments of an economy are linked together. Whether caused by the novelty of their connection to metropolitan France or the newness of the touristic phenomenon itself, local leaders simply did not understand the fragility of an economy based on tourism. The economic slowdown, they believed, would be temporary; they did not take seriously the possibility that it could last longer than one season. And so, full of confidence in Nice and in the future of tourism, the Borriglione administration embarked on ever more ambitious programs. In January 1882 a special committee, established by the municipal council to study Nice's needs, concluded that, among other things, Nice needed a new city hall, a museum, a school of decorative arts, and a new municipal theater (to replace the one that had burned down). Although none of these recommendations was immediately enacted, another scheme of the 1882 commission was. In October 1882 the administration announced that the city would soon sponsor an "international agricultural, industrial, and artistic exposition." The supporters of the show felt that it would make Nice famous in the industrial world and would attract thousands more visitors during the 1883–84 season. A sum of 200,000 francs was budgeted to support the exhibition.[10]

Unfortunately for the city, the crisis struck Nice with full force in 1883, and few visitors came to the city for the exhibition or for any other reason. The season was disastrous, and the repercussions were of a magnitude previously thought impossible. Nationwide, the free and easy prosperity of the late 1870s had led to an excess of capital, and this capital tended to find its way into ever more speculative ventures. Thousands of Frenchmen, for example, had invested their savings in Ferdinand de Lessep's ill-fated Panama Canal Company; others invested in financial paper that carried prices only remotely related to dividends. The main difference between the impact of widespread speculation on Nice and on her sister cities was that in Nice, all surplus capital went into either land or buildings. People from all classes had been caught up in the boom. As one local editor noted,

> Rich and poor, workers and property owners have, in Nice, the same system to enrich themselves: rent a corner of the sun to visitors at the highest price possible. This is the secret behind the fortunes of the wealthiest men of this city of prey where the aristocracy of the whole world comes to take up its winter quarters.[11]

Not surprisingly, Nice's real estate speculators assumed that the future would take care of itself—and of them. For a time it did, and land prices exploded at an extraordinary rate until 1883. An observer, Armand de Pontmartin, described a parallel speculative fever in nearby Cannes in 1870 in the following way:

> You have fifty thousand francs to spare—instead of gambling them at the stock exchange, buy a certain number of square meters of this privileged land. Send for an architect and a gardener and go take a walk: you return, your garden is flowering, your house gaily shows you its galleries and balconies. Go take a second walk: when you return someone will offer you ten thousand francs in profit.[12]

The newspaper *La Colonie étrangère* called Nice's builders "an invading race," moaning,

> Everyone is on the move in this land; property owners and those who would like to become property owners. The latter are struck by a terrible illness, the *disease of construction*. Oh, it is dangerous, this sickness; it can too easily result in an end, if not fatal, at least ruinous.[13]

For historians, tracing residential land values is often quite difficult.[14] Residential land, which by its very nature lacks any productive capacity, is rather like a diamond: it is worth exactly what a particular buyer is willing to pay. While the supply of residential land is certainly an important factor in determining its value, there are a number of others, too subjective, too personal, to be discerned by historians. In addition, determining land values is made more complex because the price an individual pays for his land is often one of his most closely guarded secrets, at least where official eyes are concerned. In France—where the assessment and collection of taxes is often viewed as a sport, and the goal is to outwit, confuse, and otherwise confound the tax collector— tax records are unreliable. However, whenever a land transaction is agreed upon, a local *notaire,* or "solicitor," draws up a legal document, something like a contract, detailing all of the particulars including the purchase price. Despite its official status, this document remains private and (except in unusual circumstances) is sealed to the general public for a hundred years. Thus, the temptation to misrepresent facts is greatly diminished, and the records can be considered reliable.

When the notarial records for the postannexation period in Nice are examined, the effect of the depression of the 1880s on land prices becomes clear (see graph 5).[15] As the market for building sites collapsed, prices fell precipitously, until by 1890 the price of building land was less

GRAPH 5

SPECULATIVE LAND TRANSACTIONS, 1869–1910:
NUMBER AND MEAN PRICE PER SQUARE METER

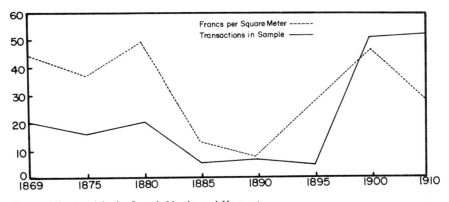

Source: Minutes of études Seassal, Martin, and Herment.

than one-fourth of its 1869 level. In 1869 one optimistic buyer had paid a record 166 francs per square meter for a lot in St.-Jean-Baptiste. This figure was not surpassed until 1900 when two parcels sold in Longchamp at a square-meter price of 172 and 182 francs, respectively.

During the depression, lots in Nice—like shares in the Union Géné-rale—had few buyers at any price. Those whose savings had not been wiped out sought safer havens for their wealth than bank stock or real estate on the Riviera. Diagrammatically, the curve of deposit levels in French savings banks is almost the reverse of the curve describing land prices in Nice. Between 1882 and 1895 savings deposits almost tripled, growing from 1.28 billion francs to 3.395 billion francs. Deposits then leveled off and did not reach 4 billion francs until 1913.[16] Chastened by the widespread losses in speculative investments, investors who in 1869 would gladly have fought for the opportunity to purchase real estate in Nice now stayed out of the market. Graph 5 shows this trend. Of the eighteen land transactions studied from 1885 to 1895, only two parcels sold for more than 20 francs per square meter. Between 1869 and 1880, however, only six (of forty-nine) parcels had sold for less than 20 francs per square meter. It was not until 1900 that land sales recovered.

Evidence of a surplus of tourist-oriented dwellings first began to surface in Nice in 1881, and the problem steadily worsened. There were five hundred unrented apartments midway in the 1881–82 season.[17] Still, construction continued, and at such a pace that one year later it was frequently said that Nice had grown so rapidly that much of it was unrecognizable. *La Colonie étrangère* observed that the city

> has undergone such development that its limits appear to have been reached. Here is a new quarter with large boulevards but no houses; in the center of the city there are numerous lots for sale which nobody wants. The beautiful city of Nice has been transformed by the fever of land speculation and can no longer be recognized.
>
> Look there: Where are we please?, the visitors ask, seeing with astonishment all this tearing up of the ground.[18]

As the financial crisis deepened, the excessive debts grew. Bankruptcies multiplied, occurring in Nice at a rate much higher than in the rest of France. Property owners were hard hit, and few of them were in a position to make even the interest payments on their mortgages. As a result, every bank suffered. For example, the Crédit Foncier, which reportedly accepted only first mortgages and never loaned more than 50 percent of the purchase price, was thought to have over 40 million francs outstanding in defaulted mortgages in Nice in 1885. That year, the economic situation had become so serious that the actual value of real property had declined to around half of what it once had been. The Crédit Foncier, like most financial institutions, had little interest in taking possession of the property on which it held mortgages. It was a bank, not a real estate agency, and had no desire "to become the holder of nearly all the houses in Nice . . . and to remain the holder of nearly an entire city."[19]

One reason for the Crédit Foncier's reluctance to assume possession of these properties was probably the way in which such speculative ventures had been built. Traditionally, the *hivernant* quarters had included large amounts of open space, planted with trees or ornamental gardens. In the 1880s, however, builders began changing their mode of construction in an effort to respond to the demands of the *mondain* tourists. It began to be common to see buildings of multiple stories, which lacked both gardens and any architectural grace. "We see buildings of five or six stories go up," noted the editor of *La Colonie étrangère*, a sun-and-air proponent. They are, he continued,

> true barracks without gardens which threaten to take from Nice its character as a watering place . . . we do not see villas of any sort, surrounded by beautiful gardens of orange trees. We need a luminous Nice, a paradise of flowers and greenery, an enchanted dream, the memory of which will be engraved on our souls.[20]

Even the sunlight had disappeared, wrote the Parisian newspaper *L'Opinion:* "It is impossible for [the sun] to penetrate the narrow streets laid out by speculators, where seven-story buildings interrupt its light on all sides." And another *hivernant* newspaper, *Le Baigneur*, complained that "in Nice there is such haste to build . . . that no one takes the trouble to do a good job," concluding that "the houses are, from this point of view, very imperfect."[21]

Although those who had invested heavily in speculative construction bore the immediate brunt of the depression, its repercussions affected the entire city. Nice's working class, of course, was heavily dependent on employment in the building trades, and workers felt the depression almost as soon as the speculators (although there continued to be some work on projects started before the crisis). Indeed, regardless of whether they had any speculative investments or of whether they were financially involved with the tourist industry, all property owners were affected.

The crisis was worsened for Nice by two underlying assumptions in the French tax system. The first was that the actual value of real and rental property was reflected in its outward appearance. The second was that the population of French *communes* (local administrative districts) was stable enough so that all new residential buildings would be constantly inhabited. French public finance has always depended heavily on impersonal taxes such as excise taxes or property taxes, assessed according to apparent value.[22] The property tax was one of France's most important taxes during the nineteenth century, and in keeping with French fiscal tradition, it focused on the potential value of real property. Assessors assigned all real property a tax based on the amount of rent that potentially could be collected on a house or apartment. In 1888 this was equal to about 5 percent of its rental value.[23]

Added together, these assessments resulted in a tax quota for which the *commune* as a whole was responsible. If a new building went up during the year, the district's tax quota increased in proportion to the potential rent. Presumably, however, the number of residents increased as well, and the amount paid by each taxpayer would remain stable. Thus, if the new building was rented, its tenants would pay the additional taxes. But if the building remained vacant, the taxes would have to be absorbed by the *commune's* other taxpayers, and everyone's payments would rise. The system was inelastic: either a decrease in the population or an increase in the number of dwellings would immediately cause taxes for all taxpayers to increase. It is easy to see that a city like Nice, where real estate speculation had become a way of life, would suffer under this system in a time of depression. By 1888 the number of vacant buildings in the city had become so great that taxes on property renting for identical amounts were 250 percent higher in Nice than in the neighboring resort city of Cannes and 400 percent higher than in nearby Grasse, home of the world's perfume industry.[24]

In addition, the ambitious projects undertaken by the Borriglione administration in its efforts to perfect Nice for the *hivernants* came home to haunt taxpayers during the depression years. The high quality municipal services that Nice had been obliged to provide its visitors had been very expensive. City administrators, of course, had argued that the improvements would attract more visitors whose expenditures, in turn, would increase receipts from municipal excise taxes enough to offset any temporary sacrifices. Events, of course, did not follow predictions; and as tourism fell off, property taxes had to make up the difference, with the rate almost doubling between 1883 and 1888 (see table 6).

The phenomenon of Nice's property taxes doubling in the face of economic difficulty is instructive. This probably did not occur in France's major industrial cities. Tourism, as the Niçois found out to their sorrow, is a volatile business and one acutely sensitive to changes in the financial climate. Although the economic collapse of the 1880s would have hurt tourism in Nice under any circumstances, the fact that the depression coincided with Nice's transition from hosting sun-and-air tourists to more worldly visitors undoubtedly worsened the crisis. These luxury-minded tourists visited an area solely to enjoy themselves; thus, the particular locale was not crucial. Furthermore they represented a fairly new phenomenon, and few had developed any lasting ties—of habit, tradition, or property ownership—in Nice. Of course, this had been predicted by supporters of the sun-and-air group who were fond of pointing out the fickleness of Nice's lively, wealthy, and mobile new guests.

Even the Casino Municipal was in trouble. Between November 1881 and October 1882, it received body blows from the dual forces of nature and the economy. The first was the most serious: in November 1881 cloudbursts over the Maritime Alps caused severe flash floods in the Paillon, damaging the casino's foundations and compromising the entire

TABLE 6
PROPERTY TAX RATES, 1883-1888

Year	Centimes per Franc of Assessed Value
1883	21.8
1884	24.1
1885	26.3
1886	34.2
1887	37.7
1888	39.2

Source: Déliberations, 12 March 1888.

project. After engineers completed a preliminary inspection, they asked the promoter to remove the gravel that had been deposited around the foundation so that the pilings could be studied. The promoter did not reply, and it was soon learned that the casino had become entangled in the general financial collapse of 1881. Eventually the casino was declared bankrupt, leaving Nice with many of the casino's financial and legal liabilities, but with none of the advantages of actual ownership, as the title to the casino was lost in a maze of legal entanglements.[25]

In many respects the casino—an unfinished, water-damaged hulk—aptly symbolized the problems of a tourist-based economy in times of national depression. Nice's leaders had become convinced that the future lay in attracting more and more wealthy visitors to the city. The city was prepared to spend huge amounts to lure them to visit on the assumption that their presence would generate increasing prosperity. Clearly, Nice's administrators underestimated the volatility of an economy based on tourism. They also underestimated the tremendous impact that speculators and shady operators of all types could have on the shape of a fast-growing city that cared only for growth. Until the 1880s few local leaders seem to have considered the possibility that one day the city would find itself in the same situation as the casino: ugly and financially embarrassed.

The financial crisis of the 1880s ushered in a period of frustration and despair. Between 1881 and 1885 acts of men and acts of God had conspired to cause nearly every ambitious project undertaken in Nice to fail; and the list of disasters is almost the same as the list of institutions designed to assure the city's future. In 1881 the Théâtre Municipal, which had stood since 1776, burned with the loss of sixty-three lives. In April 1883, the fabulous Jetée Promenade burned while being readied for its grand opening.[26] The Exposition Industrielle of 1883 attracted little attention outside Nice and was a financial failure. In 1884 a cholera epidemic struck Marseilles; and although the disease did not spread to Nice, it forced the city to quarantine all visitors for five days. In 1885 the Casino Municipal was declared bankrupt. And in the summer of 1886, in an extraordinary administrative move, the prefect of Alpes-Maritimes exercised a seldom-used power and dissolved the municipal council, appointing an interim delegation to administer the city.[27] All these events, of course, took place in the shadow of a deepening depression.

Thus, the depression of the 1880s pointed up the weaknesses inherent in Nice's economic structure and clarified the dangers associated with the second, *mondain,* stage of tourism. It also proved to all that Nice's economy had become extraordinarily sensitive—and vulnerable—to changes in the national financial climate. Although the city was geographically farther from Paris than any other major French city, financially Nice was closer than any other. Tourism had brought about this change. No amount of French propaganda or governmental encouragement could have tied Nice to France as quickly and as surely as dependence on tourism. Italian irredentism, which had flourished from time to time after the annexation of Nice, quietly faded away during the 1880s, probably because those residents whose hearts belonged to Italy realized that their pocketbooks were in France. Finally, the depression had brought home the fact that Nice had become dependent on a single industry. No other serious kind of economic activity existed that could act as a buffer when tourism failed. All municipal efforts had to be devoted to preventing the failure of tourism which had the power to make Nice one of Europe's major metropolises or to recast it as a Mediterranean village.

5

Tourism and the Problem of Public Health

ONE OF THE MOST SERIOUS PROBLEMS facing Nice during *la belle époque* was the unceasing demand of its *mondain* tourists for public services. Nice's visitors were, after all, great lovers of comfort and convenience; on vacation, they generally expected amenities superior to what they had left behind. If these amenities were not forthcoming or did not live up to expectations, the tourists were prepared to exercise their option and never return. Thus, Nice's immediate and long-range prosperity was inextricably connected to the quality of its municipal services.

In general these services fell into two categories: primary services, such as sanitation facilities and water supplies, that could only be furnished by an administrative unit; and secondary services, such as hotel and restaurant accommodations, that were supplied by private businesses and whose quality and quantity were determined by the marketplace. Providing primary services—pure water, clean streets, and an organized system of waste disposal—was the more complex task.

Although this was a serious and expensive problem for all nineteenth-century cities, it was particularly acute for a resort city like Nice that served a cosmopolitan population. Furthermore, it was complicated by two general developments. First, enormous advances had been made in bacteriology and the prevention of diseases during the last quarter of the nineteenth century. Second, during this period urban residents tended to demand more services from their public officials and to hold them accountable for inaction. These two changes, of course, were interconnected: as the discoveries of scientists such as Louis Pasteur and Robert Koch became more widely known, Europeans began to view epidemic disease as a problem that could be solved by official actions. Nice was affected more than most other cities by this desire for reform. Although its permanent population was relatively unsophisticated, the city was the winter home for many of Europe's wealthiest and most cosmopolitan

people, a number of whom were preoccupied with their fragile consti-
tutions. Partly because of their own health needs and partly because
they were in the habit of having everything around them be of the
highest possible quality, the *hivernants* insisted that Nice equip itself
with the best sanitary facilities available. Thus, Nice's administrators
were faced with the problem of reconciling these demands with the more
traditional, and less expensive, ideas of the permanent residents.

As Nice began to host more and more members of the European
aristocracy, as the city became progressively more sophisticated and luxurious, the occupants of Nice's villas and hotels began demanding improved
municipal services to match the great European cities like Paris and
London. Members of the foreign colony agreed that the time had come
to abandon the notion that Nice was a Mediterranean village and to
demand a more cosmopolitan attitude from city government on the
wholesomeness and municipal services of the city. Mayor Malausséna,
in his first major address in 1861, had remarked that "the foreign colony
. . . demands and has the right to demand much of a city for which
it is the principal support, of a city which it enlivens and enriches
every year."[1]

Besides the fact that the *hivernants* were rich, used to luxury, and
unwilling to support a city that could not provide salubrious conditions,
Nice's municipal authorities recognized other compelling reasons to
develop superior water and sanitation facilities. Because of Nice's attraction as a center for climatotherapy, many of the city's visitors cared about
problems of both private and public health and were enormously sensitive to any hint of a real or imagined epidemic. Indeed, Nice's leaders
constantly guarded against rumors that typhoid fever, cholera, or smallpox had broken out in the city. Newspapers featuring stories that dealt
with calamities in resort cities seemed to sell well, and many reports of
Riviera epidemics were published without much concern for accuracy.
Although Nice's administrators went to extraordinary lengths to combat
the impact of these false and often malicious reports regarding the public
health of the city,[2] they also realized that the only truly effective way to
counter these attacks was to convince everyone that the health of the
city was, in reality, absolutely irreproachable.

Although Nice's city fathers shared the concern of other enlightened
nineteenth-century urban administrators that their city not become a
death trap, they also found themselves in the unique position of knowing that the economic livelihood of Nice depended on keeping the city
free from disease and pestilence. As the editor of an ephemeral newspaper catering to *hivernants* pointed out in 1883:

Foreigners who come here each winter and contribute greatly to the prosperity of our city certainly have an advisory voice on questions of public health; when they wish to give advice to us, it must be thankfully received.[3]

The lesson that disease could be a tourist city's worst enemy was first learned during the great cholera epidemics that struck Europe between 1831 and 1866. Although Nice did not escape the epidemics that ravaged France before 1860, the effects on the city's economy were not too serious because of the relatively small size of the tourist population during those years.[4] The 1865 epidemic, however, which occurred shortly after the arrival of the railroad in Nice, had more serious consequences. The increased flow of traffic meant that the tourist population was much larger and more mobile and, thus, that quarantine measures would be more difficult to impose.[5]

Nice's response to the problem of epidemic disease was shaped by the medical theories in vogue during the early nineteenth century. To begin with, most experts agreed that susceptibility to cholera sprang from some kind of moral inferiority which could, under certain atmospheric conditions, cause an individual to succumb. It was thought that a cholera victim first had to have a predisposition to the disease, a condition which usually manifested itself as poverty, sexual misconduct, or immoderate eating or drinking.

For example, the sub-prefect of Lunéville, a village in northern France, noted in 1832 that respectable people should not worry much about cholera because it tended to strike "individuals of little utility to society."[6] A physician practicing in Nice during the cholera epidemic of 1835 wrote that the disease mainly attacked those "given to excesses at the table or in drinking, or certainly those who mix with the crowd, who do not eat regular meals, or who consume coarse foods." Cholera, he went on, "spreads primarily among those who live in houses which are low, damp, badly ventilated, dirty, and small."[7] Remarks such as his seemed designed to reassure potential visitors to Nice who did not fit at least the last part of his description.

The most popular explanation of the mechanism that caused the rapid but selective spread of cholera was the miasmatic theory of disease. Its proponents argued that communicable diseases arose from decaying organic matter creating miasma. Simply put, bad smells caused disease. To be sure, individual predisposition explained why some people contracted diseases and others did not, but no epidemic disease could exist in the absence of decaying matter. Epidemic diseases, therefore, could be eradicated by effectively eliminating filth, thus making it impossible for miasma to form.[8]

A second, less popular explanation for the spread of cholera was being advanced by mid century. Based on the observation that those in close proximity to a sick person often got the same ailment, the contagionist position was strengthened by important work done by medical researchers such as John Snow and William Budd. Although Snow's work is better known, both these men concluded in 1849 that cholera was caused by a specific living organism which could be transmitted from person to person by drinking water or by ingesting substances contaminated by the excreta of sick persons. Snow's study comparing the mortality rates of Londoners whose drinking water varied in the degree of pollution first established that the unknown agent that caused cholera could be transmitted through contaminated drinking water. It was not until 1883 that Robert Koch isolated the cholera vibrio and explained the mechanisms by which it was transmitted.[9]

In light of subsequent discoveries, the contagionist theory of disease is, of course, the most correct. During the middle decades of the nineteenth century, however, it was the least popular and the least accepted, and most workers in the fields of medicine and public health were anticontagionists. Although the discoveries of bacteriologists eventually destroyed the anticontagionist arguments, it was only shortly before disappearing "that anticontagionism reached its highest peak of elaboration, acceptance, and scientific respectability."[10]

Until late in the nineteenth century physicians in Nice, like those elsewhere in Europe, held divided opinions regarding the transmissibility of cholera. Some, particularly those whose opinions had been formed during the 1832 epidemic, were thoroughgoing proponents of the miasmatic theory. They were convinced that extraordinary efforts to cleanse the air of miasma through fumigation and rubbish removal could prevent cholera. Nice's contagionists, on the other hand, believed that diseases were transmitted primarily by contact with infected persons. They believed that epidemics could be prevented by the strict enforcement of quarantines, and they urged the sequestering of patients and travelers.[11]

Deciding whether cholera and other epidemic diseases were contagious was not merely an intellectual exercise. For physicians and public health officers, one's theoretical orientation defined the preventive measures to be implemented. An official who believed in the miasmatic theory would order massive clean-up campaigns designed to eliminate all decaying organic matter. News that an epidemic was approaching would trigger a flurry of street cleaning, and householders would start cleaning and fumigating their dwellings. Proponents of the miasmatic theory included Edwin Chadwick and Southwood Smith in England and J. P. Bonnafont in France. Bonnafont appeared before the Paris Academy of Medicine in 1885 and insisted that contagionists were influential only in places like Italy, Spain, and Turkey where "imagination is more honored than experience."[12] Eliminate the source of these miasma, argued the anticontagionists, and disease would disappear. Although based on erroneous assumptions, the efforts of the miasmatics to eliminate rubbish, clean the streets, and provide adequate sanitation did nothing but good. Cities were more pleasant places in which to live, and urban filth, while not the direct cause of epidemics, certainly did not enhance the general level of public health.

Contagionists, on the other hand, ignored rubbish in favor of isolating sick individuals, quarantining infected houses, and forbidding the transfer of people or goods to or from infected areas. One reason why this solution was so unappealing was its drastic impact on commerce and trade. Establishing any kind of an effective quarantine meant destroying a certain amount of individual liberty and increasing the official intervention in the lives of individuals. To be a contagionist, then, one had to be prepared to shackle trade and commerce, curtail individual freedom, and support an officious bureaucracy. It is no wonder that laissez-faire liberals of the nineteenth century rejected this solution to public health problems. Nor is it surprising that Nice's leaders often blanched at contagionism. The application of contagionist solutions would have required merciless harassment in the form of quarantines for any tourists arriving from infected areas.

The cholera epidemic of 1865 thus found Nice's leaders equipped with two contradictory theories regarding the nature of the disease. Unsure as to whether to follow the contagionists or anticontagionists, local officials applied solutions suggested by both. The first course of action was to embark on a clean-up campaign designed to rid the city's streets of miasma-producing material. In 1862 Nice had hired a private contractor to clean streets and public places. According to local custom, the inhabitant of the ground floor of a building was responsible for cleaning the street in front or for hiring the city's contractor to do it. The street-cleaner was supposed to collect all dead animals, rocks, broken dishes, broken glass, "the remains from cooking and other household garbage, straw, plants, manure, mud, and accumulated dirt."[13]

Unfortunately, the private contractor could not meet his expenses though in addition to the fees charged to individuals, he also sold the sweepings for fertilizer; and in late 1862 city officials assumed responsibility for keeping the streets clean. Municipal penny-pinching, however, ensured that the streets seldom reached the degree of cleanliness that the anticontagionists desired. Only when the cholera epidemic arrived did the city dedicate itself to sanitation, spending over four times as much on street cleaning in 1865 as it had in 1861.[14] In a final effort to combat the production of miasma, authorities tried to identify buildings where the disease had struck in the past in order to improve their salubrity. Noting that the apartments most seriously infected were "in the worst hygenic conditions that one can imagine," the city finally decided to apply the law of 13 April 1860. It allowed municipalities to inspect all buildings and to prohibit the rental of those found to be unsatisfactory.[15]

In addition to fighting miasma, Nice's leaders also adopted several contagionist solutions by trying to prevent the entry of certain travelers into the city. Not all newcomers were treated equally. Probably because the city's health authorities had observed that Nice's working classes tended to be hardest hit by disease, the quarantines usually focused on arriving laborers. As the cholera epidemic moved west from Provence in the late summer of 1865, and after the infection of Marseilles and Toulon, Nice became crowded with fleeing workers on their way home to Italy. To avoid infection, Nice persuaded the P.L.M. railroad to run special trains carrying Italian workers directly from Marseilles to Italy without stopping in Nice. Officials complained loudly that they were hampered in their work by French regulations outlawing the traditional Piedmontese practice of fumigating travelers with sulfur and creosote.[16] Like the rest of Europe, however, Nice was helpless before the onslaught of cholera. Most Niçois would probably have agreed with observations presented to the municipal council of Lyons:

> Pestilential illnesses are not those to which it is given to man to dis-
> cover the origin, or to understand their principles. All is invisible,
> mysterious, all is produced by powers which are only revealed to us
> by their effects. We must be content to accept as a fact the pestilential
> principle itself, to relate to this principle the epidemic character, the
> mode of propagation, and the terrible action of the plague.[17]

Since Nice could not afford to frighten away potential, or actual, tourists, accounts of the 1865 cholera epidemic were not generally published. However, years later, the first director of Nice's Bureau of Public Health, P.-L. Balestre, drew up statistics based on the death certificates. A glance at these figures shows why reports concerning the 1865 epidemic are scarce—it was much more serious than local officials could admit. In fact, except for 1871 when wartime economics combined with an epidemic of smallpox, the death rate in Nice in 1865 was higher than at any time between 1861 and 1911. By comparing the death rate during 1865 to the average annual mortality rate between 1861 and 1870, the devastating effect of the disease becomes apparent. Cholera caused a 24 percent increase in mortality (see graph 6). In a population of about 50,000, there were some 373 deaths due to cholera in 1865; and there were probably at least an equal number of Niçois who became seriously ill but did not die.[18]

Publicly, city officials claimed that Nice had largely escaped the ill

GRAPH 6

DEATHS PER THOUSAND, NICE AND FRANCE, 1860–1914

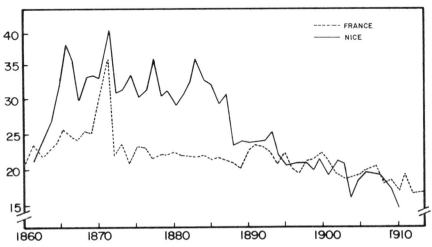

Sources: B. R. Mitchell, *European Vital Statistics: 1750–1970* (New York: Columbia University Press, 1976), pp. 106, 115; P.-L. Balestre and Edouard Grinda, *Les progrès de l'hygiène urbaine à Nice: Leur influence sur la santé publique* (Nice: Imprimerie Léo Barma, 1911), p. 3.

effects of the epidemic "thanks to the measures taken by the municipal authorities, and also, without any doubt, to our exceptional climatic conditions."[19] Unfortunately for the tourist industry, however, tourists did not agree with the official interpretation, and the 1865–66 season was a disaster. Winter visitors avoided Nice in droves. They may have decided not to come because they feared being stricken in Nice or on the general principle that it is better to be near one's home during a time of real or potential emergency. Whatever the reasons, cholera arrived in southern France in September, just as the *hivernants* were making their winter plans, and the result was a serious depression. Nice's tiny opera house, whose balance sheet was usually a good barometer of the success of the winter season, found itself in dire financial straits by November, when the season should have been in full swing. The committee appointed to study the problem reported that "this miserable situation has been caused by rumors which have been wrongly spread abroad that a cholera epidemic is raging in Nice, [that has] frightened away foreigners who usually spend the winter here." Despite management's success in persuading performers to take a 10 percent cut in salary, it soon became clear that the opera would have to close its doors unless the city provided a sizable subsidy. Although the municipal council hated the idea, it finally agreed, noting that if the opera closed, it "would completely destroy the success of the season that already has been so compromised." In April 1866 the local prefect wrote to the minister of the interior explaining that the "stagnation of business" in Nice was due to the devastating effect of the cholera epidemic on tourism.[20]

The disastrous 1865 season, then, brought home the fundamental truth that Nice's prosperity and its public health were intimately connected. Visitors would not come to an infected city, and news—or rumors—of an epidemic could make the difference between a prosperous season and a disastrous one. Clearly, if the city wished to retain and consolidate its position as "the queen of Mediterranean health spas," it would have to make Nice second to none in public health. As the city council's public works subcommittee noted ten years later, "The question of health . . . overrides all others."[21]

6

Tourism and Urban Services: Water

THE CHOLERA EPIDEMIC proved to tourists and permanent residents alike that Nice's most serious municipal problem was its precarious public health. It was equally clear, however, that no improvement was possible unless the city could transform its water supply. No amount of street sweeping or nuisance elimination could be effective without water to wash the streets, flush the drains, and otherwise wash away miasma-producing material. Besides, local leaders reasoned, supplying the city with pure drinking water would impress visitors; such cleanliness and wholesomeness were considered a luxury in most parts of Europe.[1]

Before 1864, like most other European cities not situated on a flowing river, Nice depended entirely on wells and springs for water. The Paillon, which was dry much of the year and flowed only during the winter, carrying mountain run-off into the Mediterranean, possessed a large, shallow aquifer. Over the centuries Nice's inhabitants had drilled numerous wells into this aquifer, and these, along with a handful of natural springs, had supplied the city with a modest amount of water. The quality and quantity, however, varied considerably according to the season and the location of a particular well. Nice's convent, school, and prison, as well as many private dwellings, had private wells. Public pumps served Nice's working population, although during the summer the only ones that functioned provided water which, in the opinion of the departmental chief engineer, was dangerous to drink. To solve the problem, one private company had begun in the early 1860s to deliver water from the springs of St.-Barthélémy, a community several miles away. The water, however, was expensive; and in addition, there was barely enough of it—just ten gallons per household per day, on the average—to meet the needs of those who could afford to pay.

The rest of Nice's population, some 84 percent, had to use either the polluted fountains of the port or other wells which furnished water of poor quality. In the words of one engineer, "Such a state of affairs can no longer continue without incurring the danger of seeing the end of the development of Nice."[2] The situation was critical: there was barely enough water to meet essential household needs; and during the summer, when the demand was greatest, the supply fell off. Needless to say, there was no water available for municipal sanitation.[3]

Procuring a supply of water that would accommodate the present and the future needs of the city and its residents became the top priority item on Nice's municipal agenda during the early 1860s. The tones of easy confidence that echoed throughout the meeting rooms of the municipal council usually were based on the assumption that a dependable water supply would be forthcoming. The council did not lack for suggestions as to how or where an adequate supply could be found. In general, these schemes fell into two categories: some proposed tapping springs in the Alps, north of the city; others involved using aquifers and pumping the water to a suitable level. The various proposals were studied by both local officials and national supervisory engineers to determine which would best serve the needs of the city.

Their work was shaped, of course, by municipal assumptions. First, since the new water supply was viewed as another urban feature that would enhance Nice's attractiveness to tourists, these officials insisted that the water be physically appealing, with all the purity, flavor, and softness of the best spring water. This requirement excluded using the discolored and disagreeable waters of the Var, the Paillon, or the springs surrounding the port. Second, since by the 1860s Nice had already begun to expand from its original site on the coastal plain into neighboring hills, the city's water would have to supply the highest villas. This specification also excluded those sources available around the city because they would require the mechanical elevation of water. Although proponents of these plans suggested using either water wheels or steam pumps to elevate the water, neither the engineers nor the local officials studying the proposals had much faith in mechanical contrivances and refused to make the city dependent on them for its water supply. The only solution, therefore, was to capture the necessary water in the mountains high above Nice and let it flow to the city through an aqueduct. Eventually, the departmental engineers and local authorities agreed on a proposal submitted by the Compagnie Générale des Eaux de France to tap the springs of Ste.-Thècle near the village of Peillon, some fourteen kilometers away from Nice. The water could be piped to Nice, stored in basins located above the city, and supplied to users through natural pressure.[4]

As finally presented, however, the Compagnie Générale des Eaux proposed constructing two separate systems. The first would serve those parts of Nice lying on the coastal plain, and the second would provide water to those dwellings situated in the hills surrounding the city where *hivernants* had begun building villas. The company had discovered what it thought was an underground stream, flowing beneath the Paillon, which it planned to tap near La Trinité, a village some two kilometers away from Nice. The company claimed that this system would supply at least 70 liters of water per second (and probably 100 liters), enough to serve the low-lying quarters of the city throughout the year. Water for the more elevated quarters of Nice would come from the springs of Ste.-Thècle by a series of conduits and siphons that would empty into a reservoir above the city. This system was supposed to provide at least 100 liters (and possibly 150 liters) of water per second. The two systems could, of course, be connected if necessary.

According to the company's engineers, together, the two systems were expected to supply Nice with about 15,000 cubic meters (15 million liters) of water per day. This meant that in 1866 Nice would receive 299 liters per day for each of its 50,180 permanent residents. This daily average would decrease, of course, as the *hivernants* arrived; but Nice would still be ahead of most other French cities in the amount of water it had at its disposal (see table 7). The city administration planned to

TABLE 7

WATER AVAILABLE DAILY, 1863

City	Liters per Inhabitant
Nice	300 (projected)
Dijon	240
Bordeaux	170
Paris	90
Toulouse	78
Grenoble	65
Nantes	60

Sources: Ingénieur Ordinaire de la Compagnie Générale des Eaux de France, Service de Nice, 14 November 1863; Archives Départementales des Alpes-Maritimes, S-504-1, Canal de Ste.-Thècle, Avant Projet.

use 40 percent of the water (6,000 cubic meters per day) to clean the streets and to operate public fountains. The remaining 60 percent (9,000 cubic meters) would be distributed to householders. This amount of water, said the company's proposal, "will place Nice among the most privileged of cities from the point of view of supply of drinking water." Moreover, it would fulfill "the largest needs which this city can have, from now to a time far in the future."[5]

The municipal council accepted the proposal on 24 November 1862; the stockholders of the Compagnie Générale des Eaux and the prefect of Alpes-Maritimes also approved it.[6] Local approval of a public works project was only the preliminary step, however; local and departmental officials then began the process of selling the idea to the appropriate ministries—interior, commerce, agriculture, and public works—in Paris. Without their approval neither the city nor the Compagnie Générale could exercise the right of eminent domain. Progress was very slow: one agency did not act on the proposal for sixteen months and then declared that it could not make a decision because of insufficient documentation. Final approval of the plan was not received until December 1866, long after the prefect of Alpes-Maritimes had begun firing off impatient letters to Paris.[7]

The company needed the right of eminent domain in order to take certain land owned by peasants in the region north of Nice who did not want to sell and protested the tapping of underground water. They felt that the water of the Paillon "was the private property of those living along its banks, and that they would be ruined if Nice began using its water." They feared that if Nice captured the river's underground waters, there would be none left for irrigation.[8]

The Compagnie Générale des Eaux, apparently believing that its national office, working together with the local authorities of Alpes-Maritimes, eventually would gain approval of the water project, began work without official sanction; by the time that Paris finally approved the condemnations, the company had already spent 1.5 million francs on the project. Indeed, the company was so confident of success that it began work immediately after its stockholders had approved the design. By late 1865 pipes had already been laid in the city and much of the work necessary to divert the Alpine springs had been completed.[9] The company's confidence was well founded: the official report on the project was enthusiastic and rejected all complaints. "One cannot contest," said the inspector-general, "the public usefulness of an enterprise destined to provide water to a population of more than 60,000."[10] The inspector-general's remark was more perceptive than he had imagined. After all, the estimate of 299 liters per day was based on a population of some 50,000 inhabitants. The inspector-general's estimate, which included both the permanent and the tourist population, was that each inhabitant could be provided with a maximum of 259 liters of water per day.

By 1867, Nice was no longer dependent on local wells for its water supply; and most local authorities seemed to feel that the systems developed by the Compagnie Générale des Eaux would provide Nice with clear, cool, and wholesome water for a long time to come. Although the city's pleasure was real, it was short-lived. The expensive and long-awaited Ste.-Thècle project never fulfilled expectations, both because of a massive increase in demand for water and because of inadequacies in the project's conception, design, and execution.

The first problem—the increase in demand—resulted both from the city's rapid growth soon after completion of the Ste.-Thècle project and from a greater level of consumption than had been projected. Originally, the Compagnie Générale des Eaux had made its estimates by judging consumption levels in the tradional French way—according to the outward appearance of each family. These guidelines for estimating water use are shown in table 8. A scale of fees for water then was similarly

TABLE 8

ESTIMATED DAILY WATER CONSUMPTION, 1864
(IN LITERS)

Each Person	20
Each Employee	5
Each Horse or Cow	60
Each Four-Wheeled Carriage	80
Each Two-Wheeled Carriage	40
Each Square Meter of Garden or Courtyard	3
Each Shop	150

Source: Ville de Nice, La Question des eaux, traités de 1864 à 1901 (Nice: Imprimerie Niçoise, 1912), p. 21.

developed, based on the size of each family and complexity of each household—number of bathtubs, number of horses or cows, size of garden, and so forth—without regard for actual usage.[11] The minimum fee was twenty francs per year, a big expense for Nice's laboring population: during the 1860s workers' wages in Nice averaged about two francs per day. This meant that a worker subscribing to the services of the Compagnie Générale would have to work for ten days to pay his annual water bill. In addition, of course, many laborers were engaged in seasonal or unstable occupations and could not count on a regular income.[12] Presumably they were expected, for the most part, to continue using free water, either from the old wells and springs—however disagreeable—or from the occasional public faucet which the city installed.

The cost of water was not sufficiently high, however, to deter consumption by businesses and commercial interests; nor, of course, did the cost discourage Nice's *hivernants,* especially since those who could afford water at all paid a flat rate. The Compagnie Générale made no effort to measure the amount of water actually used and followed what was called the "free faucet" policy. Thus, the *hivernants* tended to use water in large quantities to irrigate gardens and operate exotic appliances such as waterclosets and hydraulic elevators. These practices, plus the rapid increase in the overall number of consumers, produced an unexpectedly high demand for water. Thus, the Compagnie Générale's assurance that Nice's new system would meet all needs far into the future was rapidly contradicted by events. It is unclear whether the Ste.-Thècle project ever supplied anywhere near the 100 liters of water per second that the company hoped to obtain from the springs. No independent surveys were ever made in the years immediately after the project's completion. Customers who complained of low pressure and dry faucets were told by the company that it was fulfilling its obligations and that all shortages resulted from the wasteful habits of consumers. In 1902, when independent consultants examined the springs in connection with a lawsuit against the company, engineers found that the springs gave only 46 liters per second during the winter and considerably less than that during the summer.[13] Although the amount of water produced by the springs could have been depleted by fifty years of use, it is unlikely. Mountain springs are usually fed by melting snow in higher elevations, and the amount of water available is generally dependent on the amount of run-off and the size of the channels in the rock through which it must flow. Extremely light snowfall in the upper Alps could have diminished the water flow, and it is possible that the 1902 measurements reflect such a situation. Nevertheless, considering the constant complaints from Niçois throughout the 1880s and 1890s concerning the insufficiency of the water supply, the conclusions of an expert study, commissioned in 1902, were probably accurate: the Compagnie Générale never had been able to deliver the promised supply from the springs of Ste.-Thècle.

Besides its inability to supply the needs of a growing city, the Ste.-Thècle project suffered from several inadequacies in design that made it unsatisfactory from both a technical and a medical point of view. Normally, the construction of a city-wide water system decreases cholera and typhoid morbidity, lowers the overall death rate, and generally makes a city more wholesome. In Nice, only the last goal was reached. The city did have extra water to clean the streets and flush the sewers—actions which made the city much more pleasant and appealing—but the introduction of the new water systems did nothing to decrease mortality.

Although the death rate declined in 1867, shortly after the first water entered Nice, the drop was only temporary. The annual death rates in Nice from the mid 1860s to the late 1880s were very high and compared unfavorably with those of France as a whole, as well as with those of other European cities (see graph 6, chapter 5).[14]

A partial explanation lies in the composition of Nice's tourist population. Many visitors were invalids suffering from a variety of diseases which they hoped could be cured by Nice's sun and air. In many cases, however, the unfortunate visitor died instead of recovering. The records are full of the names of illustrious and not-so-illustrious visitors who succumbed while living in Nice (for example, Niccolo Paganini in 1840; the czarevitch of Russia, Nicolas Alexandrovitch, in 1865; and Marie Bashkirtsev in 1884). Tombstones in the English, Russian, and Catholic cemeteries bore mute witness to the hundreds of visitors whose last voyage had been to Nice.[15]

The main reason why the introduction of the new water systems did not reduce the death rate in Nice was the poor quality of the water itself. One must remember that the Compagnie Générale des Eaux conceived and executed its Ste.-Thècle project in the prebacteriological period, when the link between the purity of a water supply and the epidemiology of diseases such as typhoid fever, dysentery, and cholera did not exist. To be sure, most people seemed to believe that pure water contributed to good health, but the connection was intuitive rather than scientific. All agreed that if drinking water were clear, cool, inodorous, and agreeable to the taste, it was good for the drinker; whereas if it were cloudy, warm, foul-smelling, and bad-tasting, it was likely to be dangerous. This rule of thumb is not necessarily true, and the springs of Ste.-Thècle were a case in point. Although the water produced by the springs was cool, clear, and agreeable, later bacteriological analysis indicated that it harbored colonies of coliform bacteria, a sure indicator that it had come in contact with human waste. Without question the water had passed very close to human habitations higher in the Alps.[16] Nevertheless, the Ste.-Thècle water was much superior to that of the second system, obtained from the underground channel of the Paillon.

In addition to its impurity, the way in which the Compagnie Générale distributed water from these two systems furnishes another explanation for the city's high death rate. As has been noted earlier, the Compagnie Générale planned a high-pressure service, using Ste.-Thècle water, for the higher reaches of the basin of Nice and a low-pressure service using the underground stream of the Paillon, for the lower-lying areas. Water from Ste.-Thècle could always be used to supply the low-pressure service but the opposite was not possible because only gravity was used to transport the water. In essence, this meant that all of the Old City would always be served with Paillon water, while all of the villas and houses built higher on the hills around Nice would receive water from Ste.-Thècle. The net result was that Nice's visitors were, for the most part, provided with Alpine spring water while the permanent residents, most of whom lived in the Old City, were supplied with underground river water which had previously passed through a number of villages higher up in the mountains. There is no question as to which population was better served or which had the better quality water or which was likely to have the lower death rate.

Although it is perfectly clear from the documentary records that it was the intention of the Compagnie Générale's first contract with the

Washerwomen along the Paillon *(courtesy of the Musée Masséna, Nice)*

city to use Paillon water to serve the lower coastal plain, local authorities seem to have either forgotten that this was the case or tried to overlook the fact that most of Nice's permanent population were being served river water. In 1888, the president of a local property-owners' association sued the Compagnie Générale for not providing spring water to the whole city and was very indignant when the company informed him that it had been using Paillon water for twenty-two years, as was its contractual right, and did not intend to change its practices in the future.[17]

Although the Ste.-Thècle project was intended to meet Nice's water needs far into the future, it soon became clear to residents and visitors alike that new sources were needed, especially if water were to be available for purposes other than drinking and cooking. Thus, shortly after the Ste.-Thècle project was completed, the municipal council approved another major water-supply system designed to provide an additional 3,000 to 4,000 liters of water per second. This project, which was to tap the sources of the Vésubie River, was not originally intended to provide additional drinking water, although supporters hoped that it would help overcome some of the shortcomings of the Ste.-Thècle system. The Vésubie project was a simple, open canal, designed to provide water for needs other than human consumption—irrigation, sanitation, and general cleansing. The project did not receive final approval until 1878 and was not completed until 1886.[18]

The municipal council had great hopes for the Vésubie project and noted in 1870 after it had been approved locally,

> By the happy and proper success of this great enterprise our countryside, impoverished and desolated by drought, will be transformed, and our city, inundated in its promenades, its streets, its drains, and perhaps even its Paillon, will become the cleanest, healthiest, and the most prosperous in France, as [Nice] is already one of the most gracious, stylish, and most sought after.[19]

The eminent civil engineer Alfred Durand-Claye held similar sentiments about the Vésubie project. Two years before its completion he wrote, "We know of no city which at this time is endowed with such a resource." Indeed, the projected quantities of water—64,000 cubic meters (64 million liters) per day—seemed to justify this enthusiasm. As an urban hygienist, Durand-Claye was impressed. He concluded that the most serious problem Nice faced was that water by subscription was common only in the newer quarters of the city that were popular with tourists. In the Old City, municipal water entered few homes, and for most residents, public water had to be carried from community hydrants.[20]

Although the Vésubie canal was designed and approved to serve the needs of agriculture and municipal sanitation, with true entrepreneurial spirit the Compagnie Générale des Eaux (the city's concessionaire for the project) immediately began promoting alternative uses for the abundant Vésubie water. In 1884, even before the system was complete, the company used Vésubie water to operate the fountains built for Nice's agricultural and industrial exposition. At about the same time, the Compagnie Générale agreed to allow Nice's luxury hotels to use Vésubie water to operate their hydraulic elevators, even though the company's contract with the city expressly prohibited such practices. However, city officials could see no good reason why Vésubie water should not replace scarce Ste.-Thècle water to power the elevators.[21] Indeed, there was only one reason why the substitution should not have been allowed. It opened the dangerous possibility of legalizing cross-connections between the industrial and residential water supplies. No one had ever claimed that Vésubie water was suitable for drinking or cooking. It flowed unfiltered through an open canal and came from a river that had passed through several villages; and, therefore, its introduction into buildings had been prohibited in the original contract. Of course, no one intended to drink water from a canal that "received all the wastes of the villages that border the Vésubie and its branches [and which] carries dogs, cats, foxes, and other beasts that have drowned in it."[22] But by 1888 it had become clear that the motives of the Compagnie Générale were not entirely pure. When the company later was accused of installing secret cross-connections throughout the city, it argued that the substitution allowed in the hotels was a precedent.[23]

Evidence of these illegal cross-connections emerged early in 1888. When one resident of Cimiez, a suburb of Nice, complained that his water was cloudy and of poor quality, a company inspector informed him in an ill-considered remark that, in fact, Vésubie water was regularly sent to Cimiez and that the company intended to continue the practice. Furthermore, the inspector went on, "If you do not find it agreeable, you may stop your subscription."[24] By late summer the public outcry had become so great that the company, while still denying the existence of cross-connections, agreed to an independent investigation. According to the engineers' report, there was no doubt that the Compagnie Générale des Eaux had routinely mixed Vésubie and Ste.-Thècle waters during the summer when the output at the springs was low. Between 1866 and 1888 the population of Nice had grown greatly, and builders had constructed many new houses in the hills around the city; yet the yearly supply of water from Ste.-Thècle was unchanged. Clearly, the springs, which had never been particularly bountiful in the summer, could never have served so many additional people. The Compagnie Générale and city officials, who despite protestations seem to have been in collusion with the company, had to choose between supplying residents with Vésubie water and delivering no water at all in the summer. Neither of the two original systems was adequate without a Vésubie supplement; and even so, people living in upper stories often found their faucets dry. After accusing the company of incompetence, they would complain about their neighbors below, who allegedly always left their faucets on, or about wealthy landowners whose gardens absorbed all available water.[25]

While the pattern of consumption may have contributed to summer shortages, the real source of Nice's problem was elevated demand, caused both by population growth and by new assumptions regarding the quantity of water that each person had a right to consume. Nice's permanent population, after all, had grown from some 50,000 in 1866 to over 77,000 in 1886. By 1899, when Nice's population was around 100,000, the situation had deteriorated badly. Dr. E. Pilatte, a local physician interested in public health, remarked that he doubted if a typical Niçois household received more than 100 liters daily during the summer. "What kind of attention," Pilatte asked, "do you expect them to pay to cleanliness, hygiene, or even scanty clothes washing with this thin stream of water in a household of eight, ten, or even more people?" The Compagnie Générale, he added, had a moral responsibility to provide adequate service in the summer. Although technically the 1864 contract permitted the substitution of any water available for Ste.-Thècle water in case of disaster, was it not almost criminal for the company to "turn up its nose at all progress in hygiene, at all scientific discoveries, and [to] continue to distribute to a city of 100,000, to a city that lives by its healthfulness, polluted water?" "During this time," Pilatte went on,

> public health is menaced; each autumn the first rains carry millions of germs to the springs that supply us; sickness breaks out in the barracks, [and] in the poor quarters; if the wealthy quarters are not stricken, there is nothing astonishing; they are deserted and thanks to the free advertisement that makes for us, they remain empty.[26]

Pilatte clearly understood why the Compagnie Générale des Eaux had such a cavalier attitude toward the demands and complaints of Niçois during the summer. The company realized that most city officials would look the other way as long as winter visitors could be served clean, pure, and plentiful water. If the total absence of complaints registered between November and March is any guide, the company fulfilled its part of the bargain. It felt no moral or legal compulsion to provide for Nice's permanent residents during the height of summer.[27] An anonymous member of the municipal council asked in the summer of 1893 why there was often no municipal water in the Old City and why some housewives had been forced to go without water for twenty-one days. He probably knew the answer to his question: utilities existed to serve the winter visitors. As long as this was done, all was well.[28]

Although it seldom took summer complaints seriously, the company and its water-supply systems could not remain insulated from the political process forever. In August 1889 the municipal council, under pressure from residents of the Old City, decided to sue. The city won: the local administrative court ordered the company to stop furnishing water to power hotel elevators and to stop mixing Ste.-Thècle and Vésubie water. In addition, the court told officials to withhold the city's regular payments if the supply of water was insufficient. The company, dissatisfied with this judgment, appealed to France's highest administrative court (the Conseil d'Etat) in Paris. The process dragged on until 1892 when the city and the company signed a new contract. In the words of Mayor Alziary de Malausséna, the pact forced the company to provide water that would "leave nothing to be desired." However, the means by which this would be accomplished were left up to the Compagnie Générale des Eaux.[29]

Although many Niçois assumed that the new contract would oblige the company to tap new sources of spring water, the Compagnie Générale des Eaux had no such intention. Instead, it decided to take advantage of advances in water-treatment technology and to install a filter in the Vésubie system designed to precipitate the particulate matter which gave that water its distinctive, cloudy appearance. Although filtration made the water more attractive, it is hard to say whether the filter made the Vésubie water any more healthful. Before filtration, it had a microbe content forty-five times greater than Ste.-Thècle water. Local critics, led by Dr. Camous (a physician and author of a thesis on the relationship between public health and water supplies) tested filtered Vésubie water and found that the microbe content was still high for human consumption. Under the new contract, however, the city administration was helpless, and officials admitted that during the summer Niçois should resign themselves to drinking river, rather than spring, water.[30]

Besides installing the Vésubie filter, the company also attempted to balance demand by developing a complex dual water-supply system. Originally, water from the Vésubie was intended mainly for agriculture. Although the Compagnie Générale allowed and encouraged nonagricultural uses, Vésubie water lines were not permitted in private dwellings. The purpose, of course, was to prevent people from using the cheaper— impure—Vésubie water for drinking, washing, and cooking. However, as the company substituted more and more Vésubie water for that of Ste.-Thècle, many began to question the restriction. Arguments in favor of permitting Vésubie water in residences were bolstered by the increasingly widespread use of water-closets. If residents could use Vésubie water to operate these appliances, reasoned the company, large amounts of Ste.-Thècle water would become available for human consumption, as originally planned. This solution was also favored by Nice's sanitationists who assumed that the more water the city had, the healthier its residents would be.

In 1899 construction began on a large system of municipal drains designed to carry all waste water and to flush it into the sea. The system could function, however, only if sufficient water were available at all times; like modern sewage systems, it would operate properly only if each inhabitant had practically unlimited water to use in flushing his wastes away. The Ste.-Thècle water supply was plainly insufficient for these purposes.[31] Thus, in 1903 Nice signed an agreement with the Compagnie Générale des Eaux that allowed private citizens to use Vésubie water in their dwellings. Each household was required to have connections to both water systems, but Vésubie water was not to be used for anything except water closets. The two lines were not to be joined together, nor in any other way was Vésubie water to be substituted for spring water.[32] Despite the contract permitting this complicated dual system, the situation had become so serious by 1902 that an interim solution had to be found pending installation of the new pipes.

The problem, in fact, was so severe that Nice's conservative administration finally decided to put its faith in a new technology, ozone. In November 1902 the municipal council contracted with the firm of Marmier et Abraham to construct a nearby ozonization plant to purify all water delivered to the city. The ozone process had been tried only once before in France. In 1898 a purifying installation had been completed in Lille that used electricity to change oxygen into ozone which then would be bubbled through previously filtered and decanted water. Manufacturers guaranteed that the process would cleanse the water of all organisms harmful to human health and would provide 177 liters of water per day per inhabitant for a city of 200,000, Nice's winter size. Furthermore, the company was to supply 700 liters per second of untreated Vésubie water for municipal sanitation. Local officials hoped that at long last Nice would be able to implement its new sanitary regulations and permit all houses to be connected to the city drains. All municipal waste would be flushed into the sea by massive amounts of Vésubie water.[33] Recalling the foul and stagnant conditions that had typified Niçois summers since Ste.-Thècle water had first appeared, Dr. Pilatte commented that

> The foreign colony will learn with pleasure . . . that [they] can be sure that Nice's water is henceforth irreproachable and that the pathogenic *bacilli* which invade the pipes of the company at the beginning

of the summer will be seized and burned by the devouring flame of the *ozonateur*.[34]

Never again, hoped city officials, would Nice's citizens have to be advised to "boil all water during the dog-days of summer."[35]

Unfortunately for Nice's permanent residents these hopes were not immediately realized. From the beginning, local leaders viewed the water-supply network in terms of its ability to attract and retain tourists. If permanent residents benefited as well, so much the better, but neither the Compagnie Générale nor the various city administrations considered the satisfaction of the local people a primary factor. As long as an ever-increasing supply of visitors appeared each year, those responsible for the city's services felt that they had adequately done their jobs.

All of Nice's nineteenth-century water projects reflected this attitude. The Ste.-Thècle project, which was designed to provide Nice with spring water, ended by supplying it only to the tourist sections; the lower and older areas of Nice had to make do with water from the bed of the Paillon. The permanent residents who inhabited these quarters were even worse off during the summer when the supply of water from both Ste.-Thècle and the Paillon's bed dramatically decreased: then, it was back to the wells. The Vésubie canal at least allowed the Compagnie Générale to keep the city's mains full in the summer, but the water was hardly fit for humans to drink. And construction of the dual system primarily benefited those who were already subscribers to the expensive Ste.-Thècle system and who could afford water-closets or other water-intensive appliances. Residents who did not get Ste.-Thècle water benefited only indirectly insofar as the dual system decreased user-pressure on what little water Ste.-Thècle could provide during the summer. Finally, even the ozonated Vésubie water did not live up to expectations. To be sure, it was a great improvement over the unfiltered water, but the system still performed badly during the summer. As the water level in the Vésubie fell, the filters would plug with trash, and impurities would overwhelm the ozone; water pressure dropped, and sometimes was entirely lacking. Thus, many permanent residents chose to depend on nonpublic water supplies. Dr. Grinda, a local hygienist, noted the public-health dangers, saying that only when the indigenous population "renounces the deplorable use of underground water (wells, artesian wells, springs), so dangerous because of their clarity and coolness, will we no longer have water-borne diseases in Nice."[36] In the summer, the problem of water supply had improved very little for many Niçois: in 1912 a local-interest newspaper observed that a worker could seldom find enough water "to wash the end of his nose."[37]

7

Tourism and Urban Services:
Waste Disposal

THE PLENTIFUL SUPPLY OF WATER opened a new era for Nice's sanitationists and gave them opportunities undreamed of earlier. At the same time, bacteriological discoveries linked the incomplete disposal of wastes with epidemic disease, lending a new urgency to sanitary reform. Impressed by the technological, scientific, and medical advances that they had seen elsewhere, Nice's *hivernants* insisted on a rapid transformation of the city's sanitary system. Although local people were often suspicious of technological innovation, their support for sanitary improvements paralleled the tourists'—but for different reasons. Nice's leaders recognized the power of tourist demand and accepted the idea that Nice's prosperity could be compromised if they failed to respond to the new technological challenge. Thus, reforms that took decades in other Mediterranean cities, and seldom were topics for public debate, provided a main focus for Nice's public administrators.[1]

Traditionally, French cities disposed of street waste through their storm drains, the configuration of which was related to the size and location of the particular town. Small villages built on slopes usually cut channels down the middle of their streets. Larger cities sometimes built underground drains of brick or stone; usually these emptied into the nearest body of water. Solid materials deposited in them were supposed to be washed away during the next heavy rain. Unfortunately, however, many solids—such as sand from decomposing street surfaces, animal droppings, and street debris—sank to the bottom where they often refused to be washed away. Unless removed by hand, this material either generated miasma or plugged the drains. Thus, runoff often flooded dwellings and the streets.[2]

Like other French cities, Nice had equipped itself with a system of storm drains. Two separate systems existed in the Old City—one for its newer parts, near the Paillon, and another for the ancient quarters closest to the port. The former drained into the river, the latter into the sea. On the city's right bank, three storm-drainage systems were constructed, all emptying into the sea. One received water from the quarters of Carabacel and St.-Jean-Baptiste; another eliminated runoff from the central part of the plain of Nice; and a third drained the Croix-de-Marbre area. Also on the right bank, secondary collectors received runoff from most of the smaller streets.

Although efforts to provide adequate drainage in the city were sometimes energetic, one central problem always caused the solutions to be less than complete. The same dryness that made wells and springs uncooperative during the summer months caused organic matter to accumulate in the drains; there it decayed, producing obnoxious miasma. The Old City was especially plagued because during the summer the Paillon nearly dried up. Stagnant pools containing sewage and debris of all sorts formed in its gravel bed where they remained until winter, forming what the *Phare du Littoral* called "hotbeds of infection."[3]

Local officials, of course, hoped that the Ste.-Thècle water would flush the miasma coming from the drains by providing a current strong enough to dislodge sediment and carry it to the sewer outlets. After all, the famous Parisian sewers, designed by the Baron Haussmann and his chief engineer, Eugène Belgrand, were cleaned by this system, and Nice's engineers assumed that what worked in Paris would work in Nice. Like the Parisians, the Niçois were so entranced with the possibility of finally being able to clean the city's sewers that they never considered what to do with the waste water; they very quickly were overwhelmed by the disposal problems. Nice's engineers and municipal officials did not understand that supply is only one aspect of water service: whatever water goes into a city must come out. No one seems to have recognized this when the Ste.-Thècle project was being considered, designed, and executed; and only later did it become clear that the city, in solving one problem, had created another that was at least as serious. The abrupt change from having nearly all water consumed by residents to having vast quantities of it used and then disposed of was overwhelming. The problem took many years and many millions of francs to solve.

Clearly, in an age when it was generally believed that bad smells and epidemic disease were intimately connected, the Paillon constituted a real danger. The summertime situation was so serious that descriptions of the nauseating condition of the Paillon and of Nice's sewers even reached the emperor, Louis Napoléon. In a note to him the minister of the interior reported that

> in Nice they demand measures be taken to control the Paillon, which
> runs through the city, in order to eliminate the miasma which escape

from the sewers. All cities of the Mediterranean, most notably those which are located on a plain, suffer from miasma which escape from their sewers, especially when they do not possess enough water to establish a permanent flow.[4]

To solve this problem, the Niçois expanded their water supply. But in so doing, they disrupted the existing, delicate balance of urban life and found themselves face-to-face with another serious dilemma: how were they going to rid the city of waste water?

The most serious conceptual problem for Nice's leaders was their lack of experience in viewing urban services as an interconnected system. In general, a change of one part of an urban system requires a certain reorganization in other parts to establish a new equilibrium. Introducing large amounts of water into Nice had just such a disruptive effect and necessitated an adjustment in Nice's technical structures as well as in the attitudes, values, and practices of its people before the balance could be regained.

Householders, however, had no trouble deciding what to do with their waste water: they dumped it into their cesspools. Like most other mid-nineteenth-century French cities, Nice had come to depend on underground pits (*fosses d'aisance*) as their main waste-disposal system. Generally, these cesspools were lined with brick or stone and equipped with some kind of seal that was supposed to serve as a gas trap. The owner of each building was responsible for the upkeep of his cesspool and was required to ensure that it was occasionally emptied. Although administrators of most large European cities tended to view these cesspools as necessary evils, in Nice they had always occupied an important place in the regional economy. The soil of the Riviera is so poor, rocky, and unproductive that constant fertilization is essential if agriculture is to thrive.[5] Guano was expensive, and instead, farmers depended on the night soil of Nice to make their land productive. Local farmers were convinced, in fact, that night soil made better fertilizer than anything else, and neither they nor the owners of the cesspools that produced this valuable compost were willing to see Nice's traditional collection system transformed.[6]

As might be imagined, these cesspools were foul places, especially when the seals were broken. The police reports are full of descriptions of problems caused when residents fell into them. A tragic but typical incident occurred during the night of 18 July 1865, when a householder named Faraut and his son were attempting to repair the seal on their cesspool. As the father leaned over to replace the seal, he was gassed and fell in. His son cried for help and then tried to rescue his father—an effort that resulted in his own asphyxiation. Faraut's brother and wife then tried to help, and they, too, succumbed. Finally, a neighboring baker's apprentice managed to pull out Mrs. Faraut, but in the process was asphyxiated himself. When the pit finally became safe enough to enter, police found that all four persons were dead.[7] As a rule, local peasants equipped with boots, barrels, and shovels mucked out the cesspools after ventilating them and carried away the contents to their fields. By the middle of the nineteenth century, however, growth in the use of imported fertilizers, an increase in the number of residences in Nice, and a general decline in local agriculture tended to diminish both the frequency and thoroughness of the cleanings.

Although in the early nineteenth century, visitors to Nice were often annoyed by the cesspools, their distress usually was confined to times when the cesspools became too full or when the peasants made their odiferous excursions in and out of the city. At other times the cesspools were not particularly objectionable and adequately served their dual purpose of receiving wastes and providing fertilizer. The completion of the Ste.-Thècle project, however, drastically changed things. Instead of being honeycombed with relatively dry and relatively inoffensive privies, Nice now had a network of semiporous tanks filled with liquid sewage. Peasants began to lose interest in the diluted contents both because its value as fertilizer was diminished and because it was infinitely more difficult to collect and transport. And cesspools now became full more rapidly at a time when free cleaning was becoming less and less available. Almost overnight the introduction of a plentiful water supply had completely destroyed the city's complex set of linkages that had regulated sanitation. Without forethought, without planning, and, indeed, without anyone really being aware of it, technology combined with the best of intentions to overwhelm Nice's sanitary system.

Unwilling to take the unprecedented step of paying to have their cesspools cleaned, Nice's householders began searching for a cheap and easy solution. They simply connected their cesspools to the city's drainage network, using whatever piping or other materials were at hand. These connections usually were made in the top of the cesspool to carry off water whenever the tank became too full, thus allowing water and suspended wastes to flow into the municipal storm drains. Most cesspool owners made these connections very soon after they began receiving the Ste.-Thècle water in 1866. By 1871 the problem of waste water had become so serious that Nice's mayor issued a decree prohibiting such connections; but by then it was too late, and the decree could not be enforced.[8] Some years later, the secretary of the city's public works committee noted that

the existing sewers . . . have been ravaged by property owners. The contractors, while building connections [between sewers and private houses] took the easy way out and made holes in the walls of the walkways of the sewers and inserted pipes in any which direction and in any which way.[9]

During the decade following the arrival of the Ste.-Thècle water in Nice, complaints concerning the foul and obnoxious condition of the city's sewers began to appear from members of the foreign colony. They did not know why the sewers had become so foul, but they expected prompt remedial action. Nice's tourists, wrote the *Phare du littoral,* should not have to tolerate either the "loathsome odors" or the "pestilential miasma" that rose from the city's sewers and from the bed of the Paillon. In 1874, at the beginning of the winter season, the *Phare* drew up a proposal listing those improvements that it considered essential for the city. The premier item on the agenda was the elimination of the "putrid, foul water" stagnating in the bed of the Paillon near the sewer outlets. Even after the Paillon emptied into the sea, wrote the *Phare,* "miasma sicken the hearts of strollers" and threaten the health of Nice's inhabitants. In other words, the problems of the Paillon and the sewers compromised Nice's ability to give visitors what they wanted: "pure and healthful air, clean and attractive walks and boulevards, in sum a residence which satisfies them in all respects."[10]

The tourists were also troubled by the "loathsome smells" that emerged when the moist cesspools were opened. One English-speaking winterer, for example, wrote to the *Phare* complaining about the "very primitive and insalubrious method" of having farmers clean the cesspools "under the patronage of property owners who benefit from it at the cost of the repose and health of renters." Life had become intolerable, he remarked, because "the unacceptable miasma coming from the courtyard [where the cesspool was], make my apartment uninhabitable and I am sick of it, as is my whole family." This unfortunate visitor tried to cope with the problem as best he could by personally paying the cesspool's owner to hire a commercial company equipped with mechanical cleaning equipment. But, as he pointed out in his letter, he could not do this for all houses in Nice. Neither he nor his friends could understand how such practices could be permitted in a "city of luxury and of tourists."[11]

By 1875 tourists' complaints had become quite frequent. In addition, the introduction of appliances that used large quantities of water, such as the *cuvette à l'anglaise* (a forerunner of the water closet), and the widespread practice of linking cesspools to the city sewers combined to make reform of the sanitation system a necessity.[12] In facing this question, however, municipal authorities once again had to deal with the ever-present conflict between those who viewed Nice purely as a center for tourism and those who thought that the city's future depended on a mix of maritime, agricultural, and commercial activities.

Local farmers, of course, insisted on retaining their time-honored right to use the contents of Nice's cesspools to fertilize their fields even though the wastes were not as desirable as before. Shippers and merchants saw little need to sink huge sums into transforming Nice's waste-disposal system. Neither farmers nor businessmen wanted to abandon traditional practices and adopt new, untried systems simply to soothe the sensibilities of northern visitors unaccustomed to Mediterranean practices. Niçois who saw the city's future tied to tourism argued that no expense was too great if failure to spend would compromise the tourist industry. For this group, it simply was not revelant to suggest that the tourists were creating their own problems by consuming unlimited amounts of water while at the same time demanding sweet air. If sweet air, invisible sanitation, and plentiful water was what the visitors wanted, then Nice would have to give it to them. For the city to do otherwise would be criminally irresponsible. *Hivernants* and their supporters alike insisted on quick action, even if it meant spending large sums and relying on untried technology.

Thus, in 1875 the city of Nice had three choices: it could concentrate on improving its sewers so that, in one way or another, they would be adequate to carry all waste into the sea; the city could retain the traditional complex of storm drains and cesspools and attempt to make it less obnoxious; or the city could do nothing and leave sanitation in the hands of householders. This last course of action was favored by many local traditionalists who feared the expense of improvement and were not concerned with the potential dangers this plan posed for public health and for tourism. Essentially, Nice chose the middle course, retaining the general outlines of its traditional waste-disposal system and making only minor adjustments during the 1870s to take account of changed conditions. Regardless of the opinions of tourists or their local partisans, Nice's municipal council was simply not prepared in the 1870s to authorize enormous expenditures for a system of sanitary sewers dependent on a rather new technology or to abandon the interests of local agriculture. Traditional agricultural practices, financial pressure, and faith in a future when the problem could be solved without spending money or alienating traditional interests combined to convince Nice's authorities that immediate action would be precipitous.

Partly because of an unwillingness to shoulder the expense involved and partly because of their belief in the miasmatic theory of disease, Nice's leaders decided on changes that were largely cosmetic; and all their efforts were directed toward eliminating odors, rather than fundamentally altering the city's sanitary system. In 1871 the city had passed an ordinance prohibiting the connection of cesspools to the city's storm drains, but it was impossible to enforce. So the first course of action was an attempt to solve the problems caused by overflows. The municipal council argued that stagnating organic material could be removed by periodically flushing the drains with strong currents of water. Although the Ste.-Thècle water supply did not furnish enough water to do the job thoroughly, local officials believed a sufficient supply of water could be made available by shutting off the municipal fountains from time to time and by diverting the contents of municipal reservoirs built to serve Nice's abattoir. Turning off the fountains at night and during part of the day would be a small price to pay for increased wholesomeness, said Councilor Durandy, because as far as he and his committee were concerned, "the questions of cleanliness are more important than those of luxury."[13]

The second line of attack was to try to improve the way cesspools were cleaned. The ancient system of having peasants clean them during the night was clearly no longer satisfactory, and more efficient methods had to be developed. Since the city had abandoned its futile efforts to police the connection of cesspools to drains, municipal officials hoped to prevent the accumulation of solid material in the sewers by encouraging the mechanical emptying of cesspools. Unfortunately, the council's solutions were not very creative: its best suggestion involved supplying a mechanical pump to each peasant who cleaned cesspools. The council's public works committee noted that this solution would preserve the right of each property owner to sell the contents of his cesspool, maintain the supply of fertilizer, and reduce odors by speeding up the cleaning process. The committee understood the relationship between the wholesomeness of the city and the success of tourism, but their naive recommendations show how unwilling they were to come to grips with the problem. It is hard to see how giving an intensely ignorant, conservative, and suspicious peasantry mechanical pumps could have had much effect on the problem of waste disposal.[14] The committee further thought that after the system began operations, new municipal regulations could govern the construction of cesspools so that solid and liquid wastes would be separated: the liquids would flow into the sewers; and the solids would be stored in a compartment from which they could be easily excavated. This solution had been favored by Baron Haussmann, Napoleon III's prefect of Paris and the man responsible for reworking that city's urban system in the 1860s. Since Haussmann regularly wintered in Nice, it is possible that his views influenced the committee.[15]

All of these solutions, of course, were stopgap measures designed to ameliorate the conditions of the 1870s. They did not take into account the high likelihood of increased water usage and the rapid development of the new quarters on the right bank of the Paillon. Flushing the old storm drains and cleaning cesspools more efficiently was certainly a good idea, but it left the question of sanitary modernization unsolved and did nothing to build up a capital base of municipal construction on which future generations could draw. The municipal council simply thought that construction of a Parisian-style sanitation system would have been politically unpopular with local agriculturalists, expensive, and too difficult technologically to risk.

Although later generations of Niçois complained roundly about civic leaders of the 1870s who imported public water without finding a way to dispose of it, a number of factors unconnected to finances, technology, agriculture, or commerce helped shape local decision-making. The first consideration was the climate of the Mediterranean shore. Nice's unique site and climate were, of course, its main attractions to visitors who found winter there congenial, healthful, and invigorating. Although winters in Nice are mild when compared to those in London, Paris, or New York, they are far from tropical. Table 9 illustrates the general range of weather that a visitor to Nice could expect.

November through April, the months preferred by *hivernants*, are relatively pleasant with average high temperatures between 61°F and 76°F and average lows near the freezing point. Summers on the Riviera, on the other hand, are warm, sunny, and dry and are, of course, highly appealing to modern sun worshippers. Most of Nice's thirty-two inches of annual rainfall comes between November and April in hard, short storms. The same pattern of precipitation holds true for the mountains immediately to the north, although temperatures in the mountains are much cooler than those on the littoral itself. During the winter, Nice's climate is made more invigorating by the breezes that result from moist sea air meeting dry mountain air.[16]

This unique climate helps explain why the city's waste-disposal system was not as obnoxious during the tourist season as one might expect, even after the introduction of Ste.-Thècle water. Throughout the winter season, storms in the Maritime Alps and on the littoral usually provided enough water to flush the storm sewers and the Paillon; temperatures were cool enough to prevent most putrification; and the constant breezes dispersed the miasma. Local people believed that these factors allowed Nice to escape miasma-caused epidemics that would have been serious in a city with a less favorable climate.[17] Most winter residents who complained about the foulness of the cesspools or the Paillon did so at specific times of the year—in late October, early November, or

TABLE 9

WEATHER IN NICE, 1849–1861

| Daily Temperatures | | Month | Monthly Conditions | | | | |
| Mean High* | Mean Low* | | Mean Temperature* | Mean Number of Days | | | Inches of Rain† |
				Fair	Cloudy	Rainy	
66	27	January	46	17.2	7.0	6.0	2.4
62	26	February	47	16.3	6.1	5.7	2.9
66	31	March	51	18.6	6.5	5.8	2.9
76	39	April	57	16.7	6.5	6.7	2.9
79	45	May	63	17.4	6.4	7.9	2.2
80	55	June	70	19.6	5.0	5.0	1.2
88	61	July	75	23.4	4.8	2.7	1.1
88	70	August	75	23.6	4.0	3.3	1.1
91	53	September	68	17.7	5.0	7.3	2.8
76	45	October	62	17.1	6.4	7.4	3.5
75	32	November	53	15.7	6.3	8.0	5.5
61	29	December	47	18.9	5.6	5.2	3.9

* degrees Fahrenheit.
† based on 1945–1958 data.
Sources: Joseph Roux, *Statistique des Alpes-Maritimes*, 2 vols. (Nice: Imprimerie et Librairie Ch. Chauvin, 1862), 1:270–71; Raoul Blanchard, *Le Comté de Nice: Etude géographique* (Paris: Librairie Arthème Fayard, 1960), p. 81.

April. Those who arrived early or departed late registered most of the complaints; during the high-season, December through February, when rains were frequent and the temperatures cool, no one complained about Nice's sanitary state. The only nuisance was the emptying of the cesspools, a situation that could be remedied by careful cleaning and by using a disinfectant such as lime. Another mitigating factor was that in the 1860s and '70s the *hivernant* population was dispersed throughout the plain of Nice, and the low population density there decreased the probability that visitors would be bothered by the collection of night soil.

Ultimately, local actions regarding sanitary reform were governed by the same basic supposition that shaped decisions about Nice's water supply. City officials were convinced that the needs of tourists were paramount. Since the problems of stagnation in the sewers diminished during the five months of the winter season, municipal authorities chose to devote resources to projects that would have a more immediate appeal to the foreign colony.

Although the sewers and the Paillon were tolerable for most of the winter reason, during the rest of the year they must have been foul and obnoxious. The hot, dry summers with little rainfall provided an excellent climate for a city equipped with a system of dry cesspools, but after Nice began importing water from the springs of Ste.-Thècle, the climate promoted pollution and stagnation. Thus, when the *hivernants* were gone, the permanent inhabitants of Nice were treated to several months during which the organic matter in the city drains and in the Paillon stagnated with no large quantities of water available to flush it away. It must have been sickening during the summer in Nice to live near a vent or the mouth of the Paillon, and it is no wonder that few tourists arrived before mid November or stayed later than early April. The *hivernants* always claimed that the heat in Nice between April and November was intolerable, but this was a red herring: Nice's summer temperatures are really quite moderate, especially when compared to a continental climate. The sorry state of Nice's municipal services and the city's putrid atmosphere was a more probable reason for visitors' precipitous departure each April.

Thus, the overriding concern for the welfare of tourists had locked Nice into a vicious circle. By supplying visitors with more water than almost any other French city (at least during the winter), Nice, in effect, encouraged consumption and made possible the use of water-intensive appliances. Since Nice did not have a sanitary system capable of handling large amounts of waste water, native Niçois and winter residents alike vented their cesspools into the storm drains. Household wastes were flushed away in winter and left to stagnate during the summer when there was neither sufficient rain nor municipal water to wash them away. Effluvia abounded throughout the summer, and the city's miserable sanitary condition during these months probably goes far to explain the refusal of tourists to linger past April. It also probably helps explain the relatively high death rates that prevailed in the city (see graph 6, chapter 5). Unfortunately, death rates broken down seasonally and geographically are not available for this period, but it is likely that during the 1860s and '70s there was a generally elevated rate of death during the summer in the Old City and in the other sections of the city inhabited by the permanent residents.

In terms of public health, most of Nice's permanent residents clearly would have been better off if the city had made no attempt to cater to the wishes of the foreign colony. The new water supply, for example, was superb in the winter but disastrous in the summer when most of it flowed from the cesspools into the sewers, where it stagnated. Besides infecting Nice's drains, the overflow from the cesspools thoroughly polluted the city's ground water, making wells and springs dangerous to use as supplements to the municipal water supply. In short, efforts to make Nice a healthful and wholesome place to visit were successful and, combined with its unique climate, made the city a lovely and healthful place in which to spend the winter, but a less than satisfactory place in which to live year-round.

In the early 1880s, however, several events forced Nice's leaders to reconsider their conservative position. First, the economic decline precipitated by the collapse of the Union Générale bank ensured the failure of the 1882–83 season. Nice had not experienced such a season since 1870–71,[18] and the economic crisis of the '80s showed a new generation of leaders how much Nice had come to depend on tourism for its well-being. No matter how much peasants might protest, tourism clearly had become more important than agriculture. Accordingly, future discussions of sanitary reform would concentrate on the needs of the tourist industry rather than of agriculture.

Second, the transition of the tourist population helped force city administrators to take action. Visitors who came to Nice in search of sunshine, balmy breezes, and a villa surrounded with verdure were being rapidly replaced by tourists primarily interested in excitement and stimulation. Both types were wealthy and both types were prepared to make a commitment to the city, but their housing and environmental demands were different. The *mondain* tourists preferred to live in hotels rather than villas and preferred to engage in urban rather than rural activities. These worldly and energetic visitors seemed to be more familiar with new developments in technology, engineering, and medicine. Their preference for a cosmopolitan urban environment, plus their greater technical sophistication, made them more demanding of city services than were the sun-and-air *hivernants*.[19]

The third factor forcing change came from the new field of bacteriology. The early 1880s saw the discovery of the bacterial causes of typhoid fever (1880), tuberculosis (1882), and cholera (1883). A new era in public health had dawned. Although believers in the miasmatic origin of epidemic disease continued to express their ideas and tried to integrate microbiological discoveries into their theories, their days were numbered; and they were swiftly displaced by bacteriologists. During the 1880s it became increasingly difficult for city planners to believe that epidemics could be prevented by cleaning up rubbish or eliminating unpleasant odors: everything destined for human consumption had to be physically separated from wastes.

It was an unwritten rule in Nice that difficult questions of public policy were not aired during the tourist season; the new sanitation debate began after the 1883–84 season.[20] At a May meeting of the municipal council, Mayor Borriglione challenged the city and its elected representatives to squarely face the fact that the question of sanitation was of prime importance. Each year, he noted, newspapers viciously attacked the city for its alleged sanitary deficiencies. Only by imposing severe sacrifices on itself, he concluded, could the city counter the foul reputation it was beginning to gain.[21]

Action followed rhetoric, and the administration hired one of France's best civil engineers, Alfred Durand-Claye, to examine the city's sanitary system and to make recommendations for its improvement. Durand-Claye was at the height of a distinguished career: he was attached to the municipal service of the city of Paris, was professor of agricultural hydraulics at the Ecole des Ponts-et-Chaussées, and had officially advised five other cities (ranging from Budapest to Geneva) on ways to improve their sanitary systems.[22] A more eminent consultant could hardly have been obtained.

In his report Durand-Claye restated the opinion that had been put forth for decades by visitors to Nice. The city, he said, is

> incontestably the queen of the Mediterranean coast, a city where it is advisable to apply the most recent rules of modern hygiene. Nice must be proclaimed not only the most elegant, but the healthiest of our winter resorts.[23]

Durand-Claye duly took note of all of the local practices and traditions that contributed to pollution of the atmosphere, water table, and beach front: the establishment of private, illegal connections between cesspools and storm sewers, the widespread use of sewage barrels in the Old City, and the practice of venting sewers directly into the sea in front of the city. The outpouring of sewage, he wrote, "produces all along the promenade des Anglais an infection that dishonors it."[24] The solution, he concluded, was simple but not cheap: Edwin Chadwick's phrase, "circulation, never stagnation," was the key. All waste must immediately go into the sewer system, and sufficient amounts of water should be used to carry waste away from inhabited areas.[25] Unfortunately for sanitationists, Durand-Claye's report was badly timed. Faced with the problem of expanding services to the new areas recently developed by speculators at a time when tax receipts were falling, the city in 1884 was in no position to totally reorganize its sanitary system.[26]

Only in 1887 did the municipal council again return to the question of hygiene and sanitation. In March the director of the recently formed Bureau of Health, Dr. Balestre, presented an exhaustive report on sanitation. Balestre, a member of the municipal council, was a contagionist and was willing publicly to link the city's sanitary system with epidemics of cholera and typhoid fever. To him, traditionalists' arguments were absurd. The cesspool system, he wrote, which was useful only to local agriculture, was almost designed to insure "typhoid fever, cholera, and ruin." And a decrease in Nice's mortality rate, he noted sarcastically, "would certainly be worth more than several tons of fertilizer."[27] Balestre agreed with Durand-Claye that having everything flow to the drains (tout-à-l'égout) was ideally the best system, but he felt that the expense made it prohibitive. Instead Balestre proposed constructing a system of sanitary sewers made of narrow-diameter clay pipes that would parallel the storm sewers.[28] Balestre's suggestions, like preceding ones, were crippled by the fact that they ensured the loss of fertilizer. Traditionalists, as usual, recoiled from that idea. Opponents also pointed out that with water from the Vésubie to flush the sewers, the system of cesspools connected to storm drains was much improved and during the winter season was fairly odor-free. Complaints by tourists, in fact, were not as vociferous as they once had been; from the point of view of local traditionalists, this eliminated any need for rapid action.

By the 1890s, however, bacteriology had become widely accepted among Europe's educated elite, and Nice's cosmopolitan visitors seemed to be less willing to accept the thesis that an absence of bad smells ensured a disease-free environment. As L'Eclaireur de Nice pointed out in a lead article, "Questions of cleanliness are the order of the day [in] England, Germany, Holland, Belgium, and finally in France. . . ."[29] No longer could anyone contest the direct, causal relationship between inadequate underground sanitation and epidemic disease. Most important, it no longer mattered whether cesspools, sewers, and the rest of a city's sanitary system were esthetically pleasing: bad smells, while not enjoyable, had nothing to do with the incidence of cholera or typhoid fever. Thus, Nice's visitors, aware of the programs for sanitary improvement planned by the great European and American cities demanded more than simply the reduction of odors. They would not be satisfied until Europe's scientific, engineering, and medical communities were convinced of the wholesomeness of the city's sanitation system. In fact, some English tourists began employing a local English engineer to inspect their prospective dwellings to be sure they were safe from a sanitary point of view.[30]

Commenting on the necessity of having a tight, self-contained sanitation system, Mayor Alziary de Malausséna said during an interview in 1892, "I am convinced that if it is adopted Nice will be made healthy and that it will be protected from the exaggerated criticisms of the foreign colony and the foreign newspapers which greatly harmed us."[31] The mayor may well have been referring to a study of typhoid fever in Nice done by the editor of *The Lancet,* the foremost British medical journal. The results, reported to representatives of a French engineering firm, concluded that the disease

> originated principally from the contamination of the soil by the sewers. The water table, [which is] very near to the surface, is contaminated. . . . [Without a sealed system] the soil will become contaminated and I wonder then what will be the future of Nice.[32]

The man chosen in 1892 to complete a long-range waste-disposal plan for Nice was Masson, the head of Paris' sanitation service. Like Durand-Claye, this engineer believed in sending all waste to the sewers, and he recommended that Nice adopt a system similar to that used in Paris. Masson proposed dividing Nice into eight drainage sections, each of which would be served by a regional collector. These secondary collectors would carry wastes to a large main collector running under the promenade des Anglais to a point on the western edge of Nice where it would empty into the Mediterranean. Although Masson assumed that Nice's existing sewer system would become part of the new one, his plan required the extensive reworking of existing conduits, the building of reservoirs where water needed to flush the system could be stored, and siphons to carry water under the Paillon. Masson's plan also included a large steam-powered pump that would elevate the sewer water and make up for the lack of slope in Nice. In all, the new network was supposed to cost 8.4 million francs, nearly three times the city's total revenue in 1890.[33]

Mayor Malausséna was unwilling to spend this huge sum to rectify the desperate situation. Instead, he fell back on traditionalist solutions: with a stroke of his pen he signed new regulations aimed, once again, at improving the way cesspools were cleaned. Instead of having local peasants muck them out, proprietors were required to use mechanical pumping devices that would empty the cesspools without liberating their odors. In addition, householders and businessmen were required to comply with dozens of complex administrative requirements. Only the Old City, which by 1892 had become practically invisible to most *hivernants,* was excluded from these regulations; residents there remained free to clean or not to clean their cesspools by whatever means they wanted. The new regulations, however, lasted less than six weeks. On October 11, the mayor suspended them, largely because of the outrage of property owners, who refused to recognize the administration's right to regulate such a private matter as emptying cesspools, and because of the objections of local farmers, who feared the loss of fertilizer.[34]

Mayor Malausséna never revealed why he decided on such Draconian edicts which he and his advisers must have known could never be enforced. One explanation might be that he wished simply to measure the power and extent of traditionalist obstructionism and to prove to critics of the Masson plan that private solutions to Nice's sanitary problems were impossible. He also may have been worried about the attacks that foreign newspapers were launching against Nice because of its primitive sanitary facilities and may have felt that announcing strong measures, whether enforceable or not, might parry these thrusts.[35]

Despite the rescinding of Malausséna's regulations, the groundwork for sanitary reform had been carefully laid. First, detailed studies by two of France's most respected civil engineers had been completed. Second, the inability of Nice's conservative forces to solve the problem had been clearly demonstrated. Third, a public education program carried out by local newspapers had prepared the public for change. Thus, in 1893 when a special consultative commission, which included fifteen of Nice's most respected hygienists, presented a report urging transformation of Nice's sanitary system, politicians and public alike were ready for the conclusions. The committee recommended that Nice should send all wastes to the drains, abandon its cesspools, and completely renovate its drains so that the entire system would "scrupulously follow all the rules of sanitary engineering."[36] All waste water, the committee said, should flow into a single set of drains, which would empty into the Mediterranean far to the west of Nice. They urged the administration to prohibit the washing of laundry in the bed of the Paillon, a traditional practice that helped to thoroughly foul the river, and to require that all waste water from establishments such as olive presses flow directly into the municipal drains. A key to the system was a huge general collector that would run under the promenade des Anglais from the eastern side of the port to Californie, a point of land so named because of its location west of Nice.[37] The committee made no recommendations regarding the financing of the new system and did not set a timetable for its completion. It only specifically recommended sending all wastes to the drains in the newly developed quarter of Carabacel, which was more or less prepared for it.[38]

The report of this special committee marked the end of overt traditionalist opposition to sanitary reform in Nice. Sending all waste to the drains and ultimately to a collector under the promenade des Anglais remained the basis for Nice's sanitary system. Although work proceeded in fits and starts, Nice never departed from the high sanitary standards it had set for itself. Gradually, Nice's administrators overcame conservative opponents of public sanitation, procured the enormous sums necessary for completing the system, and, through the visible impact of their work, convinced tourists that Nice was a wholesome and salubrious place to winter. Incidentally, of course, these reforms made it a place visitors could enjoy during the summer as well. Opponents of public sanitation came to agree with remarks made by A. Balestre in 1892. "Nice lives by its wholesomeness," he said. "It has the duty, if it wants to keep the brilliant place that it now occupies, to install all modern improvements."[39]

Conclusion

ANY EFFORT TO EXAMINE the history of a great city must of necessity be incomplete, and the first task facing an urban historian is to choose those aspects of a city's development that illustrate both its uniqueness and its typicality in terms of the general process of urbanization. I have chosen to focus on the structural and physical development of Nice as it grew from a drowsy Mediterranean town to one of France's largest and most cosmopolitan cities. Specifically, I am interested in the organization of an urban economy based on tourism, the interaction between Nice's permanent residents and its winter visitors, and the conditions surrounding the delivery of basic city services. Some questions, such as those involving services, are general ones, similar to those faced by other nineteenth-century cities. Other questions are specific to a tourist town. Yet, whether specific or general, the problems associated with urban development were defined more precisely in Nice than in other cities because they always were resolved with an eye toward the reaction of tourists who demanded much from the Queen of the Riviera.

Clearly, the most important fact of life in Nice was the tourist population itself. Its presence hung over the city like a cloud, casting shadows on all aspects of urban life. No political, economic, or administrative decision could be made without considering its potential impact on the city's visitors. Nice was ruled by an invisible presence able to exact terrible penalties if its demands were ignored. Nice's leaders found themselves required to interpret a will which, if misinterpreted, had the power to destroy them. Thus, urban institutions in Nice can only be understood when examined in light of their relationship to the demands of the tourist population and in reference to the powerful conditioning force of the tourist industry. In some cases, tourism shaped Nice's development by directly influencing the city's leaders; in others, tourism shaped the city's evolution by subtly imposing itself on the everyday

125

decisions made by ordinary residents. All questions ranging from the installation of sanitation systems to workers' choices of residence were, in one way or another, linked to the powerful and pervasive forces generated by the tourist population. Gradually, the entire economy of the city became tied to the tourists, and every person who bought or sold property, erected a building, or took a job found himself guided by tourism's invisible hand.

From this perspective, the political realities of providing and administering basic services in Nice were unique, although the technological problems were not. Each time a decision regarding the design of the city, its urban infrastructure, or the allocation of its municipal resources had to be made, Nice's leaders found themselves compelled to evaluate the impact of their choices on the future success of the tourist industry. If these men erred, disaster was possible. If they succeeded in correctly interpreting or predicting tourist demand, the probability of the city's continued prosperity increased, although outside factors such as a national financial crisis or a war could still intervene. In general, between 1860 and 1914, Nice's leaders succeeded in correctly interpreting the future needs of the *hivernants* even though they often despaired when outside forces kept winter residents away.

Local leadership was further complicated by changes in the composition of the tourist population. Nice's early visitors were largely in search of a resort with warm sun and clear air, where a compromised state of health could be repaired. They wanted to rest and to relax, and they demanded only peace and quiet from their hosts. As the tourist city matured, however, visitors arrived with far different tastes. These people were more attuned to the active enjoyment of life and wealth, and they cared only for the city's ability to entertain them. This transition made enormous demands on the city; and Nice's leaders, terrified about a future without tourists, milked the city's resources to satisfy their every whim, whether real or imagined.

The effort to anticipate future tourist demands and to fulfill current ones warped the outlook of Nice's leaders. As the city tried to shape itself into a form conducive to tourism, it became more and more dominated by outsiders. Nice's leaders came to think that the city's resources—its urban space, municipal facilities, and municipal revenues— were primarily useful in attracting visitors. Sometimes, as in the case of water supply, when those quarters of the city inhabited by permanent residents were systematically shortchanged, the discrimination was blatant; in other cases, it was merely less visible. Nonetheless, favoritism toward Nice's winter residents was always there. Municipal services are scarce resources and are always allocated according to some official view of where political and economic power lies. In Nice's case, municipal administrators were absolutely convinced that their main official responsibility was to attract and retain visitors, regardless of the expense; and every effort was made to insure that the winter residents would return again and again.

To study the internal development of Nice, then, is to study a city whose social, political, and economic life was shaped by outsiders. It also means studying a city in which internal political systems operated in an aura of unreality. Whether from the Old City or the New, mayors and council members alike knew that once in office the needs of their constituents would become secondary to those of nameless outsiders.

Although officials occasionally tried to disguise this fact, it really was no secret to anyone familiar with the decision-making process in Nice. Nice's upper and middle classes, in particular, were perfectly aware of these tourist-oriented policies and of their implications for permanent residents. Recognizing the imperatives underlying the city's administrative policy, these people naturally tended to associate themselves with the tourist population as much as possible, in order to share the resources showered on the tourists. Insofar as it was physically possible, the upper and middle classes tried to create an identity of interest between themselves and the *hivernants*. The most graphic expression of this can be seen in their tendency to inhabit the same geographic space. Recognizing that municipal resources followed the tourists, Nice's upper and middle classes followed them too, effectively isolating themselves from the city's other permanent residents. Thus, in the same way that tourism shaped the attitudes of Nice's officials, it also shaped the social, occupational, and residential structure of the city: by 1914 the Old City had become a cultural and social island.

The arguments surrounding Nice's internal development soon were eclipsed by international strife. At first viewed as an unfortunate event, the assassination of Archduke Ferdinand in Sarajevo rapidly assumed the gravest international importance. Tensions between the two great European power blocs, which had been smoldering for years, suddenly exploded. One after another, the European powers honored their treaty commitments and mobilized their armies. By early August the European world was at war. On August 4, the day the British cabinet sent its ultimatum to Germany, Sir Edward Grey, the foreign secretary, gloomily stared out of his window as the gaslights were being extinguished. "The lamps are going out all over Europe," he observed. "We shall not see them lit again in our lifetime." Nice, a self-proclaimed city of light and luxury, painfully learned the truth of Grey's statement.

At first the news of war was little noticed in Nice. Late July, after

127

all, was a time of rest for most Niçois. The hotels were closed, and no tourist parasols shaded the city's streets and boulevards. Indeed, the trial of Mme. Caillaux (the wife of Joseph Caillaux, a Radical-Socialist and former prime minister), accused of killing an unfriendly newspaper editor, captured as much space in the *Eclaireur de Nice* as did Austria-Hungary's declaration of war on Serbia.[1] Mme. Caillaux's murder trial, however, was quickly forgotten; the war was not. It transformed Nice.

Unlike the Franco-Prussian War, whose effects were severe but short-lived, World War I had a drastic impact on Nice. The 1914–15 season, naturally, did not materialize. The French army requisitioned many of the great hotels, and instead of welcoming tourists, those grand structures housed wounded Allied soldiers and the medical units that cared for them. The army made little effort to maintain the requisitioned hotels: furniture was shifted from one hotel to another; no inventories were kept of requisitioned materials; and because the state paid no rent, there was no money after the war for renovation. The requisitions were a terrible blow to many hotels; many of them never fully recovered.[2]

The war also transformed Nice's clientelle. Tourism of the type popular during *la belle époque* became a casualty of war. Many of the vast fortunes that had fueled the tourist industry disappeared—victims of wartime taxes, postwar inflation, and revolution. The free-spending Russians, for example, once a mainstay of Nice's economy, disappeared entirely or returned as penniless émigrés. Other members of the international leisure class found themselves unable to sustain their prewar life-styles; and although Nice made valiant efforts to reestablish the season, it never achieved its prewar éclat. The displacement of *mondains* by more modest visitors, the introduction of paid vacations for workers, and the development of a summer season combined to place enormous demands on Nice's resources and required a complete reorientation of the city's economic structure. A new age had dawned for Nice, an age that often made the free-wheeling, free-spending tourism of *la belle époque* seem like another world, a world of dreams.[3]

Notes

INTRODUCTION

1. H. Robinson, *"Aspect" Geographies: A Geography of Tourism* (London: McDonald and Evans, 1976), pp. xxiii–xxiv.
2. Two French historians who have done pioneering work in the history of tourism are Louis Burnet, whose *Villégiature et tourism sur les côtes de France* (Paris: "Bibliothèque des guides bleus," Librairie Hachette, 1963) is extremely valuable, and Marc Boyer, who has written extensively on the history of tourism.
3. Burnet makes a valiant effort to distinguish between *villégiature* and tourism: in his opinion, *villégiature* implies rest while tourism implies movement. This distinction is useful when comparing post–World War II tourism to its earlier antecedents, but in this work, which does not extend beyond 1914, the terms will be used more loosely. See Burnet, *Villégiature et tourism,* p. 10.
4. Raoul Blanchard, *Le Comté de Nice: Etude géographique* (Paris: Librairie Arthème Fayard, 1960), pp. 71–81.
5. *La Colonie étrangère,* 9 February 1882, p. 1.

CHAPTER 1

1. Robert Latouche, *Histoire de Nice,* 3 vols. (Nice: Ville de Nice, 1951–65), 1:57–61; Ernest Hildesheimer, "Nice au milieu du XVIIIᵉ siècle: Rapport de l'intendant général Joanini," *Nice historique* 71 (1968):33–51, 80–95, 126–32.
2. Latouche, *Histoire de Nice,* 1:57; Hildesheimer, "Nice au XVIIIᵉ siècle," pp. 131–32. See also A. Demougeot, "Présentation et texte d'un mémoire sur le commerce de Nice (1747–1749)," *Recherches régionales (Côte d'Azur et contrées limitrophes)* 9, no. 2 (1969):15–31.
3. See map 237, "L'Industrie au milieu du XVIIIᵉ siècle," in Edouard Baratier, Georges Duby, and Ernest Hildesheimer, *Atlas historique: Provence,*

129

Comtat Venaissin, Principauté de Monaco, Principauté d'Orange, Comté de Nice (Paris: A. Colin, 1969). This map does not include information on primary enterprises such as oil pressing.

4. Fernand Braudel, *The Mediterranean and the Mediterranean World in the Age of Philip II*, vol. 1, trans. Siân Reynolds (New York: Harper & Row, 1972), pp. 41–43. This volume is the first English edition of Braudel's 1966 revision of his masterful work.

5. Arthur Young, *Travels during the Years 1787, 1788, & 1789 Undertaken More Particularly with a View of Ascertaining the Cultivation, Wealth, Resources, and National Prosperity of the Kingdom of France,* 2d ed., 2 vols. (1794; facsimile ed., New York: AMS Press, 1970), 1:199.

6. Ibid., 1:205; Robert Latouche, *Histoire du Comté de Nice* (Paris: Bovin, 1932), p. 155; and Robert Latouche, "La Situation économique et politique du Comté de Nice pendant les premières années de la Restauration Sarde (1814–1823)," *Nice historique* 24 (1926):45.

7. The Duke of York, for example, a younger brother of George III, stopped in Nice in 1764. Latouche, *Histoire de Nice,* 1:69; Jean-Jacques Antier, *Le Comté de Nice* (Paris: Editions France-Empire, 1970), p. 256; Henri Tschann, "Nice, capitale mondiale du tourisme," in Jean Médecin et al., *Livre du centenaire du rattachement de Nice à France* (Nice: Imprimerie Meyerbeer, 1960), p. 103.

8. Tobias Smollett, *Travels through France and Italy,* vol. 5 of *Miscellaneous Works of Tobias Smollett,* 4th ed. (Edinburgh: Sylvester Doig and Andrew Stirling, 1811), pp. 427–30.

9. Voltaire (François-Marie Arouet) to Jean-Claude Philibert de Trudaine, 1777, quoted by André Merquiol, *La Côte d'Azur dans la littérature française* (Nice: Editions Jacques Dervyl, 1949), p. 68; A.-L. Thomas to Madame Necker, 28 December 1782 and 22 October 1784 in A.-L. Thomas, *Oeuvres complètes,* vol. 6 (Paris: Verdière, 1825), pp. 382, 422.

10. François-Emmanuel Fodéré, *Voyage aux Alpes-Maritimes ou Histoire naturelle, agraire, civile, et médicale du Comté de Nice et pays limitrophes,* 2 vols. (Paris: F. G. Levrault, 1821), 2:257; Joseph Price to Archbishop of Canterbury (John Moore) 26 April 1792, Vicar Generals' Papers, Lambeth Castle Library, London (this information was kindly provided by the late Professor Robert W. Greaves).

11. According to the Bills of Mortality of 1796 for London, approximately 5,264 deaths out of a total of 17,648 (30 percent) were caused by lung diseases. A 1918 study based on the Bills of Mortality indicates that this was not extraordinary and that deaths caused by tuberculosis in London gradually increased throughout the eighteenth century, reaching a high point sometime between 1780 and 1830; there is every reason to believe that this pattern was reflected in other European areas. See M. W. Flinn's excellent introduction to his edition of Edwin Chadwick, *Report on the Sanitary Condition of the Labouring Population of Great Britain* (1842; reprint ed., Edinburgh: Edinburgh University Press, 1965), pp. 11–12.

12. Fodéré, *Voyage aux Alpes-Maritimes*, p. 257; see also Jean Ducoeur, "Cent ans de climatothérapie à Nice," *Le Mémorial de Nice, 1960* (Nice: Editions de l'Armanac Nissart, 1961), p. 269.

13. Latouche, *Histoire de Nice*, 1:69; Merquiol, *La Côte d'Azur*, p. 57; Victor-Emmanuel Seguran, *Les Rues de Nice: Chroniques historiques et descriptives sur le vieux et le nouveau* (Nice: Imprimerie Gauthier, 1888), p. 54; Young, *Travels*, 1:200.

14. Daniel Faucher, ed., *La France: Géographie-tourisme*, 6 vols. (Paris: Librairie Larousse, 1951), 6:299; Alain Decaux, *Les Heures brillantes de la Côte d'Azur* (Paris: Librairie Académique Perrin, 1964), p. 31; Charles de Brosses, *Lettres historiques et critiques sur l'Italie*, 3 vols. (Paris: Ponthieu, 1798), 1:43; Young, *Travels*, 1:196–200. Young's route was much the same as that chosen by most eighteenth-century tourists who customarily followed the old Roman road passing through Marseilles, Toulon, Le Luc, Fréjus, Antibes, and Nice; see map 29, "Préhistoire du tourisme (fin du XVIIIe siècle)," in Baratier et al., *Atlas historique*.

15. Jean Fourastié and Françoise Fourastié, *Voyage et voyageurs d'autrefois* (Paris: Denoël, 1972), p. 16; Daniel Féliciangeli, "La Développement de Nice au cours de la second moitié du XVIIIe siècle: Les Anglais à Nice," *Annales de la faculté des lettres et sciences humaines de Nice* 19 (1973):58.

16. A. Barety, "Le Voyage de Nice d'autrefois: d'Antibes à Gênes par la route," *Nice historique* 15 (1913):169–85; Ernest Hildesheimer, review of Denis-Michel Andréis, "Le Traité Franco-Sarde de 1760, Origines et conséquences" (Mémoire de Maîtrise, U.E.R. Lettres et Sciences Humaines de Nice, 1971), *Recherches régionales (Côte d'Azur et contrées limitrophes)* 12, no. 1 (1972): 55–64.

17. A. Pietri, "Nice capitale touristique," *Actes du quatre-vingt-troisième Congrès National des Sociétés Savantes, Aix-Marseille, 1958, Bulletin de la section de géographie* (Paris: Imprimerie Nationale, 1959), p. 225; Christopher Hibbert, *The Grand Tour* (London: Weidenfeld and Nicolson, 1969), p. 72; Barety, "Le Voyage de Nice d'autrefois," p. 169.

18. Marc Boyer, "Hyères, station d'hivernants au XIXe siècle," *Provence historique* 12 (January 1962):143–44; Max Gallo, "Pour une étude de la santé publique à Nice sous l'administration Sarde: Enquête sur le choléra à Nice en 1835," *Recherches régionales (Côte d'Azur et contrées limitrophes)* 5, no. 3 (1965):50; Decaux, *Les Heures brillantes*, pp. 67–71; Pierre Borel, *Côte d'Azur*, trans. Alan Ramsay (London: Nicholas Kaye, 1957), p. 99; Victor Sardou, "Nice et Cannes en 1840," in F. D'Ustrac et al., *Nice-exposition* (Paris: Imprimerie A. Labure, 1884), p. 56. Cannes grew so rapidly after Brougham's arrival that it soon lost its sleepy character: in 1867 he and a number of his fellow *hivernants* petitioned the minister of public works for the construction of sidewalks along Route 7 to accommodate pedestrians endangered by "incessant" traffic (Archives Nationales [hereafter cited as A.N.], F^{14}1684).

19. See Sardou, "Nice et Cannes en 1840," p. 46; Antier, *Le Comté de Nice,* p. 261.
20. A. L. Millin, *Voyage en Savoie, en Piémont, à Nice et à Gênes,* 2 vols. (Paris: C. Wasserman, 1816), 2:83–85; J. Suppo, "Les Vieux noms de rues à Nice," *L'Eclaireur de Nice,* 19 November 1907, p. 4.
21. Millin, *Voyage,* 2:84.
22. Louis Roubaudi, *Nice et ses environs* (Paris: Allonard, 1843), p. 45.
23. Abbé Expilly to C. F. Scheiffer (ex-Swedish ambassador to France), 23 June 1780, quoted in Jean-Jacques Hemardinquier, "Nice à l'heure du despotisme éclairé: Lettres et mémoires de l'Abbé Expilly," *Actes du quatre-vingt-dixiéme congrès national des sociétés savantes, Nice, 1965: Section d'histoire moderne et contemporaine,* 3 vols. (Paris: Bibliothèque Nationale, 1966), 1:272; A.-L. Thomas to Madame Necker, 12 November 1782, in A.-L. Thomas, *Oeuvres,* 6:359–60.
24. Latouche, *Histoire de Nice,* 1:44; S. Papon, *Voyage dans le département des Alpes-Maritimes, avec la description de la ville et du terroir de Nice, de Menton, de Monaco, etc.* (Paris: Imprimerie de Crapelet, 1804), p. 10; Seguran, *Les Rues de Nice,* p. 11; Antier, *Le Comté de Nice,* p. 261. The term "right bank" refers to the western part of Nice, closest to France, and the term "left bank" refers to the eastern part, closest to Italy.
25. Latouche, *Histoire de Nice,* 1:82–84; Latouche, *Le Comté de Nice,* pp. 176–81; Decaux, *Les Heures brillantes,* p. 38.
26. A. Demougeot, "Les Anglais à Nice pendant la paix d'Amiens, 1802–1803," *Recherches régionales [Côte d'Azur et contrées limitrophes)* 3, no. 1 (1963): p. 34.
27. A.N., F⁶II, Alpes-Maritimes 4. "Extrait des procès verbaux des séances du Conseil Général du Département des Alpes-Maritimes, Séance du 27 fevrier 1810." The location of the Dépôt de Mendicité is given in *Guide des étrangers à Nice 1858–59 publié par l'office central des étrangers* (Nice: Imprimerie Canis, 1858), p. 122; Latouche, "La Situation économique et politique du Comté de Nice," p. 45.
28. A.N., FˡᶜIII Alpes-Maritimes (Ancien Département) 3. Châteauneuf-Randon, prefect of Alpes-Maritimes, to Citoyen Jean Chaptal, minister of the interior, 20 Brumaire An II (11 November 1802); Demougeot, "Les Anglais à Nice," p. 35.
29. Edouard Scoffier and Felix Blanchi, *Le "Consiglio d'Ornato" 1832–1860* (Nice: Imprimerie Meyerbeer [1960]), pp. 38–48; Ernest Hildesheimer, Le Développement de Nice depuis deux-cent-cinquante ans," *Le Charactère saisonnier du phénomène touristique: Ses conséquences économiques* (Aix-en-Provence: La Pensée Universitaire, 1963), p. 59.
30. Latouche, *Histoire de Nice,* 1:118; *L'Eclaireur de Nice,* 24 November 1912, p. 4. This kind of planning was rare in Europe in the first half of the nineteenth century. For example, in 1841, after reading a report on the medical condition of handloom weavers, the Englishman Nassau Senior wondered, "What other result can be expected when any man who can purchase or

hire a plot of ground is allowed to cover it with such buildings as he may think fit, where there is no power to enforce drainage or sewerage, or to regulate the width of streets, or to prevent houses from being packed back to back, and separated in front by mere alleys and courts?" *Report of the Commissioners on the Condition of the Hand-loom Weavers,* Parliamentary Papers 10 (1841):73, quoted by Flinn, "Introduction" to Chadwick's *Report,* p. 39.

31. André Compan, "La Société Niçoise en 1860," *Nice historique* (Numéro spécial du centenaire) 63 (1960):59.

32. F. A. Brun, *Promenades d'un curieux dans Nice* (Nice: Imprimerie et Lithographie Malvano-Mignon, 1894), p. 117.

33. Latouche, *Histoire de Nice,* 1:118; Borel, *Côte d'Azur,* p. 158.

34. Latouche, *Histoire de Nice,* 1:126–29.

35. For estimates of the tourist population see: Roubaudi, *Nice et ses environs,* p. 353; Paul Canestrier, *Nice terre de France: Essai historique* (Rodez: Imprimerie P. Carrere, 1940), p. 100; Decaux, *Les Heures brillantes,* p. 79; *L'Eclaireur de Nice,* 2 October 1910, p. 1; Paulette Lèques, "Tourisme hivernal et vie mondaine à Nice de 1860 à 1881: Cercles et salons," *Annales de la faculté des lettres et sciences humaines de Nice* (1973), p. 96; Latouche, *Histoire de Nice,* 2:146.

36. *Guide des étrangers à Nice 1858–59,* p. 7.

37. Prosper Mérimée à Viollet-le-Duc, 17 December 1856, in Prosper Mérimée, *Lettres à Viollet-le-duc (documents inédits 1839–1870),* vol. 1 of *Oeuvres complètes de Prosper Mérimée* (Paris: Librairie Ancienne Honoré Champion, 1927), p. 26.

38. Most of the above details can be found in Latouche's *Histoire de Nice,* 1:124–34, although he places greater emphasis on what he calls "spiritual affinities."

39. See Edgar Holt, *The Making of Italy, 1815–1870* (New York: Atheneum, 1971), pp. 204–25, for a readable and concise account of this episode.

40. Quoted by François Malausséna, mayor of Nice, in a speech before the municipal council of Nice; see Registres des Délibérations du Conseil Municipal de la Ville de Nice, Séance du 11 March 1861. The minutes of the council's proceedings are conserved in the Archives Municipales de la Ville de Nice; they are cited hereafter as Délibérations.

41. Ibid.

CHAPTER 2

1. Between 1850 and 1870 France's rail network grew faster than that of either the United Kingdom or Germany. See J. H. Clapham, *Economic Development of France and Germany 1815–1914,* 2d ed. (Cambridge: Cambridge University Press, 1923), p. 339.

2. Gaston Imbert, *Esquisse de l'activité économique des Alpes-Maritimes*

(Nice: Chambre de Commerce de Nice et des Alpes-Maritimes [1959]), p. 83. The P.L.M. could extend its services east of Toulon only after receiving financial guarantees from the national government. The rapidity with which the decree granting eminent domain was signed after Villafranca illustrates the importance that the imperial government placed on the rapid completion of rail links to France's new territory. See René Tresse, "L'Etablissement de la voie ferrée dans l'arrondissement de Grasse, 1852–1882," *Revue d'histoire économique et sociale* 47 (1970):355–56.

3. Imbert, *Esquisse de l'activité économique*, p. 83.

4. Délibérations, 5 July 1861; Josette Martini, "L'Avenue de la gare à Nice," *Recherches régionales (Côte d'Azur et contrées limitrophes)* 3, no. 3 (1963): 14.

5. Délibérations, 5 July 1861.

6. It is possible, of course, that all these arguments concerning the location of the station were irrelevent and that the only factor considered by the P.L.M. was its ability to minimize its losses. The P.L.M. might not have believed that enough visitors would ever be attracted to Nice to make its dead-end line pay for itself. If that were the case, the P.L.M. probably would have tried to locate the station and tracks on the cheapest land available and to avoid passing through any part of the city whatsoever. The P.L.M., therefore, could have cloaked its economic designs in the arguments of Nice's protourism faction. While discussing the development of the British rail system, H. J. Dyos noted that "almost every yard of projected line pressed against some obstacle" and that a line constructed for political, rather than economic, reasons would have had every reason to avoid all potentially expensive obstacles (Dyos and D. H. Aldercroft, *British Transport: An Economic Survey from the Seventeenth Century to the Twentieth* [Leicester: Leicester University Press, 1969], p. 180).

7. A.N., F^{14}8829, Mémoire du comte de Beaurepaire de Souvagny, 4 December 1869.

8. Merquiol, *La Côte d'Azur*, p. 132; Patrick Howarth, *When the Riviera Was Ours* (London: Routledge and Kegan Paul, 1977), pp. 33–34.

9. Imbert, *Esquisse de l'activité économique*, p. 83.

10. Most of these estimates were made by contemporary observers and were published at the time: see *La Chronique niçoise*, 8 March 1867, p. 2; *La Chronique des stations hivernales*, 1 October 1867, p. 2; *Le Phare du littoral*, 18 June 1881, p. 2; also see Latouche, *Histoire de Nice*, 2:146. Alexandre Lacoste gives the figures for total arrivals by rail in *Nice, pittoresque et pratique* (Nice: S.-C. Cauvin, 1876), p. 157; Lèques, "Tourism hivernal et vie mondaine," pp. 93–101.

11. Délibérations, 27 May 1871.

12. Raynaud did not discuss the reasons for the obvious decline that had taken place in agriculture, commerce, and manufacturing, but it probably was caused by competition from commodities brought by rail from other parts of France. Grain produced in Nice's arid climate could not compete with

cereals raised in the Ile de France; the silk and sail-cloth industries could not compete with the factories of Lyons and Marseilles; and Nice's port certainly could not compare favorably with those of Toulon and Marseilles. Clearly, the completion of rail links was a mixed blessing. Délibérations, 19 December 1877.

13. Archives Départementales des Alpes-Maritimes (hereinafter cited as A.D. des A.-M.), 1M1, Poulan, maire adjoint, to Raguet de Brancion, Prefect of Alpes-Maritimes, 4 June 1879.

14. *La Colonie étrangère*, 9 February 1882, p. 1.

15. A.N., F^{1e}III, Alpes-Maritimes (nouveau département) 2, Minister of the Interior, compilation of information gathered from various sources regarding construction in Nice prepared for the files [1862]; and Prefect of Alpes-Maritimes, Denis Gavini de Campile, to the Minister of the Interior, 7 November 1862.

16. The amount of tax collected on doors and windows varied with the importance of the city. For a city the size of Nice, the tariff ranged from about .8 francs per opening for buildings with one opening to 1.5 francs per opening for buildings with more than six openings; openings used for commerce or for the entry of carriages were assessed a tax of 15 francs. Thus, both the number of openings and the size and use of the buildings influenced this tax. When increases in the revenues from this tax outstripped the increase in numbers of openings, it was a sure indication that larger and/or more luxurious buildings were being built as well as a sign of greater commercialization. See Maurice Block, *Statistique de la France comparée avec les autres états de l'Europe,* 2 vols. (Paris: Amyot, 1870), 1:374; A. Siffre and M.-H. Siffre, "L'Evolution de la richesse dans le département des Alpes-Maritimes de 1880 à nos jours," *Nice historique* 77 (1974):11.

17. A.N., F^{5}II Alpes-Maritimes 7-9^4. Budgets, An VII [1798] à 1904.

18. Délibérations, 15 January 1882.

19. Ibid., 8 August 1872; A.N., F^{12}4481 Alpes-Maritimes, Prefect of Alpes-Maritimes to the Minister of Commerce [1886]; Département des Alpes-Maritimes, *Rapport du préfet et annexes, Conseil Général, Session de 1875* (Nice: Imprimerie Canis, 1875), p. 143.

20. Robert de Souza, "Un Plan régulateur: Comment l'établir?" *L'Eclaireur de Nice,* 2 April 1910, p. 1.

21. The streets which formed the old belt boulevard are the present-day boulevards de Carabacel, Dubouchage, Victor Hugo, and Gambetta.

22. Raymond Cotto, "Cent ans d'architecture à Nice," in *Le Mémorial de Nice, 1960* (Nice: Editions de l'Armanac Nissart, 1961), pp. 283–84; A.N., F^{1e}III Alpes-Maritimes (nouveau département) 2, Minister of the Interior, Memorandum concerning building in Nice [September 1862].

23. De Souza, "Plan régulateur," p. 1.

24. Délibérations, 3 May 1861.

25. *L'Eclaireur de Nice,* 24 November 1912, p. 4.

26. Délibérations, 24 November 1862.
27. Ibid.
28. Between 1860 and the present, this main artery has had four different names: under the Second Empire it was avenue du Prince Impérial; with the fall of the Empire the street received the prosaic name avenue de la Gare. The street was named avenue de la Victoire after World War I and has recently received the name avenue Jean Médecin.
29. Délibérations, 27 April 1864; 23 May 1864; 24 March 1865.
30. Quoted by M. Fébvre, a municipal council member; see ibid., 30 December 1913.
31. Ibid., 4 December 1865.
32. Sam B. Warner, *Streetcar Suburbs: The Process of Growth in Boston, 1870–1900* (New York: Atheneum, 1969), p. 37.
33. H. J. Dyos, *Victorian Suburb: A Study of the Growth of Camberwell* (Leicester: Leicester University Press, 1961), p. 79.
34. Latouche, *Histoire de Nice,* 2:140.
35. Délibérations, 22 February 1880; J. Durandy, *Notes sur le plan régulateur des quartiers de St. Philippe et de la Buffa* (Nice: Imprimerie et Lithographie Niçoise, 1880), p. 7.
36. The plan for St.-Jean-Baptiste was updated and expanded in 1844 and 1858; see Délibérations, 17 August 1864.

CHAPTER 3

NOTE: A portion of this chapter was previously published as "The Population Dynamics of a Tourist City: Nice, 1872–1911," *Proceedings of the Third Annual Meeting of the Western Society for French History,* ed. Brison D. Gooch (College Station, Tex.: The Western Society for French History, 1976), pp. 421–27.

1. *La Chronique niçoise,* 23 December 1866, p. 2; *Le Phare du littoral,* 13 February 1874, p. 2.
2. *La Chronique niçoise,* 8 March 1867, p. 2.
3. *Le Phare du littoral,* 25 September 1872, p. 2; 20 November 1870, p. 1. The *Phare* was referring to Garibaldian irredentism in this context. Garibaldi who had been born in Nice, was furious at Cavour's willingness to cede Garibaldi's home to France, and desperately wanted to make it part of a united Italy. Indeed, Garibaldi was so angered by the cession of Nice that he considered leading his Red Shirts north instead of south in 1860. France's military defeats in 1870 and the Italian annexation of Rome in the same year aroused hope among irredentists of Nice that a defeated France, coupled with an aroused Italy, would create a situation whereby they would once again become Italian. See Holt, *Making of Italy,* p. 233.
4. *Le Phare du littoral,* 9 September 1875, p. 2.
5. Donald Jay Grout, *A Short History of Opera,* 2d ed. (New York: Columbia University Press, 1965), p. 499; Délibérations, 1 July 1872.

6. Délibérations, 30 September 1872; 11 November 1872; 10 February 1873; 14 May 1873; 1 July 1872.
7. *Le Phare du littoral,* 1 December 1871, p. 2.
8. A.N., F¹ᶜIII, Alpes-Maritimes (nouveau département) 2, Commissaire central de police de Nice to the Minister of the Interior, 18 February 1863; *Nice indicateur: Guide de l'étranger à Nice* (Nice: Imprimerie Niçoise, 1893), pp. 16–17.
9. *Nice indicateur,* pp. 16–17; Latouche, *Histoire de Nice,* 2:164–69. Armance Royer, "Cent ans d'administration municipale à Nice," in *Le Mémorial de Nice,* p. 77. The custom of employing semiprofessional specialists to build huge parade floats decorated with cut flowers seems to have been first established in Nice, as was the practice of judging the floats and awarding prizes based on size, extravagance, and imaginative use of flowers.
10. For a general discussion of prostitution in nineteenth-century French society, see Theodore Zeldin, *France: 1848–1945,* vol. 1, *Ambition, Love, and Politics* (Oxford: Clarendon Press, 1973), pp. 304–14.
11. A.D. des A.-M., M-23, Petition to the Prefect, 15 June 1863; Commissaire Spécial de Police à Villefranche to the Prefect of Alpes-Maritimes, 7 March 1865; Délibérations, 29 May 1871.
12. *La Chronique niçoise,* 23 December 1866, p. 2.
13. Délibérations, 21 November 1873.
14. *La Chronique des stations hivernales,* 20 October 1876, p. 1; Edmond Planchet, "Monte-Carlo," *Revue des deux mondes* 55 (15 January 1883): 451.
15. Latouche, *Histoire de Nice,* 2:154–55.
16. Délibérations, 20 December 1875.
17. Ibid., 8 July 1876.
18. See Latouche, *Histoire de Nice,* 2:113–26 for a discussion of Borriglione and his work.
19. Délibérations, 9 September 1879.
20. Remarks of M. Rand, secretary of the special commission created to study the projected covering of the Paillon. The commission was composed of the members of the regular public works and finance commissions. Délibérations, 9 September 1879.
21. Ibid., 5 March 1875; 16 November 1875; *La Chronique des stations hivernales,* 17 October 1876, p. 1.
22. These figures were all extracted from Nice's municipal budgets; see Archives Municipales de Nice (hereafter cited as A.M. de Nice), *Budgets de la Ville de Nice pour l'exercice de . . . (1861–1910).* In 1910 the expenditures for public holidays included:

	francs
horse racing	200,000
airplane racing	100,000
carnival	40,000
spring horse racing	35,000

yacht racing	17,000
Bastille Day	8,000
publicity for the city	5,000
rowing competition	4,000
automobile races	3,000
unforeseen expenses	2,000

The supplemental budget also provided 3,000 francs for a Golf Club, 1,500 francs for a Lawn Tennis Club, and 1,000 francs for a Bicycle Club.

23. It would be hard to find a group that better illustrated Thorstein Veblen's remarks concerning "conspicuous leisure" and "conspicuous consumption" than Nice's *mondain* tourists (*The Theory of the Leisure Class: An Economic Study of Institutions* [New York: New American Library, 1953], pp. 41–80). Although Veblen did not specifically refer to tourists, one recent effort to develop a sociology of tourism has relied in part on his thesis: see Dean MacCannell, *The Tourist: A New Theory of the Leisure Class* (New York: Schocken Books, 1976).

24. Latouche, *Histoire de Nice,* 2:148.

25. Lèques, *Tourisme hivernal et vie mondaine,* pp. 96–101. Queen Victoria of England, although hardly a *mondaine,* wintered in Nice for many years, staying first in the Grand Hôtel and then in the Regina Palace (see Howarth, *When the Riviera Was Ours,* pp. 69–74).

26. See Jean Devun, "L'Evolution de Nice de 1860 à 1960," *Recherches régionales (Côte d'Azur et contrées limitrophes)* 10, no. 4 (1970):13–20. Devun reports that by 1913 Nice possessed 130 jewelry stores, making it second only to Paris among French cities.

27. Those occupations added to the category of "day laborer" include workers calling themselves "peddler," "common laborer," "shop boy," "bill poster," etc. This process illustrates the advantages of using computer analysis on nominative census data. A researcher is not tied to the categories used by census officers and, instead, can combine them in such a way as to maximize their meaning. If, for example, one were faced with a modern census that included categories listing filling-station attendants, grocery baggers, and car-wash attendants, it would be appropriate under some circumstances to combine them. This would be impossible to do, however, for any geographic unit other than the one for which the original aggregations were made unless nominative-level data were used. For a discussion of the methodology employed in this analysis, see Sources.

28. Day laborers in Nice led difficult lives. The severity of their lot struck the United States consul in Nice, who described it for the benefit of the secretary of state:

Common laborers who make and carry mortar get 40–45 sous per day. They begin work at 5 A.M., at 8 A.M. they stop half an hour for breakfast—then work till noon. From 12 to 2 P.M. they rest and eat dinner; . . . they work as long as they can see—making 12 and a half hours of work per day. *They board themselves* [emphasis in original]. For breakfast they have bread and butter,—perhaps an onion, or a piece of cheese and half a litre (a pint) of vin ordinaire. Dinner the same. At night a cheap soup for supper. The common laborer counts himself lucky to get meat once a week. The masons get meat once a day. The wine is very light—pour sour stuff—costs six sous a litre. Peasants, farm laborers, get no better wages than ordinary day laborers in town. Nothing here strikes an American more forcibly than the difference in living between the laborers here and at home.

A. O. Aldis to Secretary of State William H. Seward, 24 June 1867, in Dispatches from the American Consul-General at Nice, National Archives, Washington, D.C.

29. This group includes brick masons, carpenters, plumbers, and cabinet makers.

30. This category includes physicians, dentists, hotel and restaurant professionals, businessmen, landlords, entrepreneurs, investors, pharmacists, and legal professionals.

31. After Nice's annexation to France, all residents of the city were asked to choose between French and Italian citizenship. The pressures were great, of course, for them to become French, and many of them declared their allegiance to France under real or imagined duress.

32. See C. James Haug, "Manuscript Census Materials in France: The Use and Availability of the *Listes Nominatives,*" *French Historical Studies* 12 (1979):258–74.

Chapter 4

1. A.N., $F^{12}4481$, Prefect of Alpes-Maritimes to the Minister of Commerce, s.d. [1886]. The prefect estimated that between 35,000 and 40,000 workers were occupied in construction, a figure that seems somewhat high.

2. Délibérations, 15 January 1882; *La Colonie étrangère,* 17 November 1881, p. 2.

3. François Caron, *An Economic History of Modern France,* trans. Barbara Bray (New York: Columbia University Press, 1979), p. 53; Jean Lescure, *Crises générales et périodiques de surproduction,* 2d ed. (Paris: J.-B. Sirey, 1910), pp. 148–50; Rondo Cameron, *France and the Development of Europe, 1800–1914: Conquests of Peace and Seeds of War* (Princeton: Princeton University Press, 1961), p. vii.

4. *Revue des deux mondes,* 16 June 1881, p. 957; Caron, *Economic History,* p. 65.

5. Jean Bouvier, *Le Krach de l'Union Générale, 1878–1885* (Paris: Presses Universitaires de France, 1960), pp. 129, 140, 230–31.

6. Ibid., pp. 142–44, 184, 218.

7. Léon Say, "La Politique financière de la France," *Journal des économistes* 20 (15 November 1882):159. Wholesale prices in France actually began falling in 1878 after twelve years of relative stability; by 1887 they had declined 23 percent. The depression was not confined to France, and price levels in both Great Britain and Germany behaved in a similar way. As usual, deflation was accompanied by unemployment, business failures, and

sluggish economic performance. See Shepard B. Clough and Charles W. Cole, *Economic History of Europe,* rev. ed. (Boston: D. C. Heath, 1946), pp. 662–63.

8. These proportions are based on the manuscript census schedules of 1872 and 1891.

9. *La Colonie étrangère,* 25 November 1882, p. 2.

10. *Délibérations,* 15 January 1882; 30 December 1882.

11. *La Chronique niçoise,* 23 December 1866, p. 2.

12. Patrick Legrand and Odile Legrand, "La Rue d'Antibes et le quartier de la croisette à Cannes," *Annales de la faculté des lettres et sciences humaines de Nice* (1976), p. 163.

13. *La Colonie étrangère,* 3 November 1881, p. 2.

14. Useful guides on land values include: Philippe Vigier, *Essai sur la répartition de la propriété foncière dans la région alpine, son évolution des origines du cadastre à la fin du second empire* (Paris: S.E.V.P.E.N., 1963), pp. 15–57; Jean Bouvier, "Sur les dimensions mesurables du fait financier: XIX et XX siècles," *Revue d'histoire économique et sociale* 46 (1968): 161–84; Paul Gonnet, "Archives fiscales et histoire urbaine," *Revue d'histoire économique et sociale* 35 (1957):41–51; Paul Gonnet, "Archives fiscales et histoire sociale," *Revue d'histoire économique et sociale* 36 (1958):432–43; Adeline Daumard, "Une Source d'histoire sociale: L'Enregistrement de Paris en 1820 et 1847," *Revue d'histoire économique et sociale* 35 (1957): 52–78; Gabriel Désert, "L'Enregistrement: Source d'histoire sociale," in *Actes du quatre-vingt-dixième congrès national des sociétés savantes, Nice, 1965: Section d'histoire moderne et contemporaine,* 3 vols. (Paris: Bibliothèque Nationale, 1966), 1:33–53.

15. Of the six notaries in Nice, three deposited most of their pre-World War I records in the Archives Départementales des Alpes-Maritimes. I was allowed to consult these records with the generous permission of Maîtres F. Desmaris, C. Lefebvre, and J.-C. Desmaris (étude Seassal—up to 1899); Maîtres T. de Poulpiquet de Brescanvel, Charles Martel, J. Benne, and J.-C. Freschel (étude Martin—up to 1910); and Maîtres M. Aral, P. Mouzon, and E. Azuelos (étude Herment—up to 1900). Scholars are hardly ever permitted access to these records, and I extend my warmest thanks to these gentlemen.

It was not possible to examine every land transaction, so I sampled the records at five-year intervals, selecting 176 land sales between 1869 and 1910. (I chose 1869 instead of 1870 on the grounds that transactions recorded during *l'année terrible* would be so abnormal as to be of little comparative use.) In picking this sample, I excluded agricultural land (rural, sold in large parcels, for no more than two francs per square meter), land with villas (because sale prices would be distorted by the buildings), and land too vaguely described to locate or to calculate the size of the parcel.

16. B. R. Mitchell, *European Historical Statistics, 1750–1970* (New York: Columbia University Press, 1976), p. 690.

17. *La Colonie étrangère,* 24 November 1881, p. 2; 22 December 1881, p. 2.

18. Ibid., 4 November 1882, p. 2.
19. Ibid., 10 January 1885, p. 1; Clapham, *Economic Development*, p. 384.
20. *La Colonie étrangère*, 4 November 1882, p. 2.
21. Ibid., 21 February 1885, p. 1 (reprint of *l'Opinion* article); *Le Baigneur*, 22 June 1884, p. 2.
22. These regressive and relatively inflexible taxes were firmly entrenched in France where the idea of a tax on income was viewed with extreme distaste. For a brief description of attitudes toward income taxes in the nineteenth century, see William L. Shirer, *The Collapse of the Third Republic: An Inquiry into the Fall of France in 1940* (New York: Simon and Schuster, 1969), pp. 87–88.
23. Ernest Lairolle, *Etude sur la contribution mobilière à propos de son augmentation progressive à Nice* (Nice: Imprimerie Victor-Eugène Gauthier, 1888), pp. 13–14.
24. Délibérations, 12 March 1888. The depression affected Cannes much less than Nice, probably because most of its visitors were sun-and-air people, many of whom had abandoned Nice because of its *mondain* atmosphere.
25. *The Méditerranean: Gazette des étrangers*, 16 November 1882, p. 1; 8 December 1882, p. 1; A.D. des A.-M., S-461-3, Minister of Agriculture, Direction de l'Hydraulique Agricole to the Prefect of Alpes-Maritimes, 21 June 1886.
26. *Le Phare du littoral*, 25 March 1881, p. 1; *La Colonie étrangère*, 7 April 1883, p. 1.
27. Délibérations, 9 April 1881; 26 June 1885; 9 May 1886; A.D. des A.-M., M 3ième République 39, Rapport du Gendarmerie à M. le Préfet des Alpes-Maritimes, 5 April 1883.

Chapter 5

1. Discourse of Mayor François Malausséna, Délibérations, 11 March 1861.
2. For example, in 1892 Dr. Balestre, in an effort to counter attacks in the press outside Nice, wrote an open letter signed by some twenty-five of the consuls and vice-consuls residing in Nice, assuring the public of the city's excellent sanitary state. See letter of 19 January 1892 published in *The Méditerranean: Gazette des étrangers*, 7 February 1892.
3. Ibid., 3 April 1883, p. 2.
4. One direct result of the outbreak of the 1830s, however, was Lord Brougham's "discovery" of Cannes; it became the preferred destination for many English *hivernants* and, hence, a competitor to Nice.
5. Most historians of medicine view the rapid spread of Asiatic cholera in the nineteenth century as a result of improvements in transportation: the incubation period of cholera is very rapid. In an age of slow ships and few passengers between India and Europe, transmission of the disease is unlikely; for cholera to become epidemic, the movement of large numbers of people is required, and one can view the rapid spread of the diesase within

Europe and America as resulting from the ease of travel by rail. See George Rosen, *A History of Public Health* (New York: MD Publications, 1958), pp. 276–77.

6. Quoted by George D. Sussman, "Carriers of Cholera and Poison Rumors in France in 1832," *Societas—A Review of Social History* 3 (1973):251.

7. Gallo, "Pour une étude de la santé publique," p. 43.

8. Erwin H. Ackerknecht, "Anticontagionism between 1821 and 1867," *Bulletin of the History of Medicine* 22 (September-October 1948):562–93.

9. Rosen, *History of Public Health,* pp. 278–89; Flinn, "Introduction" to Chadwick's *Report,* pp. 62–63.

10. Rosen, *History of Public Health,* p. 289; for evidence of a gradual move toward the contagionist position, see Rosenberg, *Cholera Years,* pp. 75, 164, 195.

11. Gallo, "Pour une étude de la santé publique," pp. 47–49.

12. P.-P. Bonnafont, *Le Choléra devant l'Académie de Médecine: La Contagiosité et les quarantaines* (Paris: Librairie J.-B. Ballière, 1885), p. 16.

13. Délibérations, 17 February 1862.

14. The municipal budget for street cleaning rose from 5,000 francs in 1861 to 22,000 francs in 1865; see A.M. de Nice, *Budgets de la Ville de Nice.*

15. Délibérations, 24 November 1865; 4 December 1865.

16. Ibid., 7 September 1865.

17. M. Candy, *Rapport sur le choléra-morbus de Paris (epidémie de 1849) présenté à M. le maire et au conseil municipal de Lyon au nom d'une commission médicale* (Lyon: Imprimerie de Radanet, 1849), p. 17.

18. P.-L. Balestre and Edouard Grinda, *Les Progrès de l'hygiène urbaine à Nice: Leur influence sur la santé publique,* XV^{ieme} Congrès National de la Propriété batie, Nice, 3–11 Avril 1911 (Nice: Imprimerie Léo Barma, 1911), p. 3. This estimate was made by applying morbidity rates observed in Paris during previous epidemics; there, of those ill enough to enter a hospital or consult a physician, about half succumbed: see M. F. Blondel, *Rapport sur l'épidémie cholérique 1853–54 dans les établissements dépendant de l'administration générale de l'assistance publique de la Ville de Paris* [Paris: Imprimerie de P. Dupont, 1855], p. 120.

19. Remarks of the prefect before the Conseil Général des Alpes-Maritimes in Département des Alpes-Maritimes, *Rapport du préfet et annexes, conseil général, session de 1866* (Nice: Typographie de V.-Eugène Gauthier, 1866), p. 17.

20. Délibérations, 27 November 1865; A.D. des A.-M., M 29, Prefect of Alpes-Maritimes, Denis Gavani de Campile, to the Minister of the Interior, 4 April 1866.

21. Délibérations, 19 May 1875.

CHAPTER 6

1. In 1850, for example, Britain's General Board of Health charged the com-

panies that supplied London with providing water of inferior quality—
so hard as to be almost worthless for domestic use, full of organic matter,
and polluted with the city's sewage. See Simon, *English Sanitary Institutions,* p. 220.

2. A.D. des A.-M., S-504-1, Rapport de l'ingénieur ordinaire de la Compagnie Générale des Eaux de France, Service de Nice, 14 November 1863.

3. A. Pietri, "Le Paillon, Torrent de Nice: Essai d'étude d'un cours d'eau des préalpes méditerranéenes" (abrégé de la thèse soutenue devant la faculté des lettres et des sciences humaines d'Aix-Marseille, le 30 avril 1955), p. 16; A.M. de Nice, 126 0 103, Rapport de l'ingénieur en chef des Alpes-Maritimes sur les mesures à prendre pour l'alimentation des fontaines publiques de la ville de Nice, 3 July 1863; A.D. des A.-M., S-504-1, Rapport de l'ingénieur en chef des Alpes-Maritimes sur l'établissement de la distribution d'eau de la ville de Nice, 10 April 1866.

4. A.M. de Nice, 126 0 103, Rapport de M. le comte Grandchamp, Ingénieur en Chef des Ponts et Chaussées, Alpes-Maritimes, 24 February 1864.

5. A.D. des A.-M., S-504-1, Rapport de l'ingénieur ordinaire de la Compagnie Générale des Eaux de France, Service de Nice, 14 November 1863.

6. Ibid., Directeur de la Compagnie Générale des Eaux to the Prefect of Alpes-Maritimes (Denis Gavini de Campile), 2 April 1864; Prefect of Alpes-Maritimes to the Minister of the Interior, 15 April 1864.

7. Ibid., Prefect of Alpes-Maritimes to the Minister of the Interior, 29 May 1865 and 22 October 1866; Minister of the Interior to the Prefect of Alpes-Maritimes, 2 June 1865 and 11 August 1865; Minister of Agriculture, Commerce, and Public Works to the Minister of the Interior, 1 December 1866; Rapport du Conseil Général des Ponts et Chaussées, 19 November 1866.

8. Ibid., Petition signed by numerous inhabitants of the *quartier* of St. Roch to the Prefect of Alpes-Maritimes, 6 October 1864.

9. Ibid., Rapport du Conseil Général des Ponts et Chaussées, 19 November 1866; Département des Alpes-Maritimes, *Rapport de l'Ingénieur en Chef, Conseil Général des Alpes-Maritimes, Session de 1864* (Nice: Typographie de V.-Eugène Gauthier, 1864), p. 56. See the same reports for the sessions of 1865 (p. 51) and 1866 (p. 27); and Département des Alpes-Maritimes, *Rapport du préfet et annexes, Conseil Général, Session de 1867* (Nice: Typographie de V.-Eugène Gauthier, 1867), p. 128.

10. A.N., F¹⁴12392, M. l'Inspecteur Général des Travaux Publics à Nice to the Minister of Agriculture, Commerce and Public Works, 24 June 1865.

11. Compagnie Générale des Eaux de France, *Traités avec la ville de Nice pour la distribution des eaux de Sainte-Thècle* (Nice: Imprimerie spéciale du "Petit Niçois," 1895), p. 26.

12. Joseph Roux, *Statistique des Alpes-Maritimes,* 2 vols. (Nice: Imprimerie et Librairie Ch. Chauvin, 1862), gives much information concerning labor and production in Nice; see 2:344–45 for wages of various occupations.

13. Edouard Grinda, *La Question des eaux à Nice: Projet d'alimentation de*

la ville en eau potable par les sources du Vegay et de la Gravière, com-pletées par les eaux de Ste.-Thècle et da la Vésubie. Discours prononcé à la séance du conseil municipal du 27 mars 1912 (Nice: Imprimerie de l'*Eclaireur*, 1912), p. 4.

14. Balestre and Grinda, *Les Progrès de l'hygiène urbaine à Nice*, p. 3.

15. For a touching description of some of these cemeteries, see Mrs. Robert Henrey, *Milou's Daughter Madeleine: A Sentimental Journey to the South of France* (New York: E. P. Dutton, 1955), pp. 167–70.

16. Grinda, *La Question des eaux*, p. 35.

17. Ibid., pp. 9–10, 24.

18. Latouche, *Histoire de Nice*, 2:136.

19. Délibérations, 15 July 1870.

20. Ville de Nice, *Assainissement de la ville de Nice: Rapport de M. A. Durand-Claye* (Nice: Imprimerie Nouvelle, 1884), p. 8.

21. A.M. de Nice, 111 0 103, Ingénieur de la ville de Nice to M. le Maire de Nice, 6 June 1888; Délibérations, 20 August 1888.

22. *L'Eclaireur de Nice*, 13 July 1888, p. 1.

23. The Compagnie Générale was authorized to substitute Vésubie water for Ste.-Thècle water only if the Ste.-Thècle canal were to break. There was one authorized cross-connection, to which the city had the only key, for use in such an emergency: Délibérations, 20 August 1888.

24. *L'Eclaireur de Nice*, 15 March 1888, p. 1; A.M. de Nice, 2 0 103, Report of M. Fouquet, professional engineer, 9 October 1888; Délibérations, 12 March 1888.

25. *L'Eclaireur de Nice*, 30 August 1893, p. 1; 25 July 1894, p. 1; *Notice sur l'état de la question des eaux en août 1901* (Nice: Imprimerie Langoise [1901]), p. 5.

26. *L'Eclaireur de Nice*, 2 August 1899, p. 2.

27. In 1895 the city administration prepared a map describing complaints of residents who had no water at all one day in August 1895: there were no complaints from the suburbs north of the railroad tracks or from the suburb of Baumettes to the west of the city; residents of the older quarters, however, registered 126 complaints. This striking discrepancy could be explained either by the unlikely total abandonment of these suburbs by the permanent residents who lived there or by the fact that these suburbs were served by the Ste.-Thècle system which always had been superior. See Grinda, *La Question des eaux*, pp. 131–32.

28. Délibérations, 5 September 1893.

29. Ibid., 30 August 1889; 22 December 1890; 19 April 1892.

30. Ibid., 20 August 1888; *L'Eclaireur de Nice*, 20 August 1898, p. 2. Ste.-Thècle water contained 4,000 microscopic organisms per liter; Vésubie water, 180,000.

31. Délibérations, 24 July 1899.

32. Ville de Nice, *La Question des eaux, traités de 1864 à 1909* (Nice: Imprimerie Niçoise, 1912), 1:123; Délibérations, 18 April 1903.

33. Délibérations, 26 February 1909.
34. *L'Eclaireur de Nice,* 21 November 1902, p. 1.
35. Ibid., 12 August 1908, p. 1.
36. Ibid., 24 July 1909, p. 1.
37. *Le Bien de Nice,* 26 August 1912, p. 1.

CHAPTER 7

1. For descriptions of sanitary conditions in other southern French cities, see:
   A. Armengaud, "Quelques aspects de l'hygiène publique à Toulouse au
   début du XXe siècle," *Annales de démographie historique,* 1975, pp. 131–38;
   Pierre Guillaume, *La Population de Bordeaux au XIXe siècle: Essai
   d'histoire sociale* (Paris: Armand Colin, 1972), pp. 13–20; Gaston Rambert, *Marseille, la formation d'une grande cité moderne: Etude de géographie urbaine* (Marseilles: Imprimerie du *Sémaphore,* 1934), pp. 416–20.
2. J. C. Wylie, *The Wastes of Civilization* (London: Faber and Faber, 1959),
   p. 46; Chadwick, *Report,* pp. 113–15.
3. Délibérations, 19 May 1875; *Le Phare du littoral,* 3 November 1874, p. 3.
4. A.N., F^{Ie}III Alpes-Maritimes (nouveau département) 2, Minister of the
   Interior, note pour l'Empereur [August 1862]. The minister was quoting
   a letter he had received from the prefect of Alpes-Maritimes, dated 4 August 1862 [same dossier]. Although there is no way to prove whether Louis
   Napoleon actually read the memos concerning Nice, it seems likely that
   he did, given his intense desire to see that the Niçois were pleased with
   their new nationality.
5. J. Fenart, "Etude économique de l'agriculture dans les Alpes-Maritimes,"
   Recherches régionales (Côte d'Azur et contrées limitrophes), vol. 4, no. 1
   (1964):3.
6. In Nice each apartment traditionally came with a barrel into which the
   chamber pots and all other household wastes were emptied. Full barrels
   were replaced by empty ones and carried away by local peasants. At all
   hours of the day, one could meet these peasants ambling through the city
   with dripping barrels on their shoulders or tied to the backs of donkeys.
   The local peasants paid for the privilege of emptying household barrels
   and, like buyers of fruits, vegetables, or precious metals, insisted on knowing exactly what they were paying for. Fodéré, that intrepid observer,
   remarked that Nice had a public employee whose job was probably unique
   in the world: his sole duty was to grade the night soil and to assess penalties against those who sold theirs without first having it graded. Local
   peasants agreed that the quality of night soil diluted with dishwater or
   other adulterants was inferior, as was that of families living on poor diets
   (see Fodéré, *Voyage aux Alpes-Maritimes,* 2:30–36). Even religion made
   a difference: "The wastes of Protestants, who are always fat," noted A. L.
   Millin, "are worth more than those of good Catholics, who are often lean"
   (*Voyage,* 2:104).

7. A.D. des A.-M., M-28, Chef d'Escadron Commandant des Alpes-Maritimes to the Prefect of Alpes-Maritimes, 18 July 1865.

8. *Le Phare du littoral,* 20 August 1871, pp. 2–3; Ville de Nice, Commission consultative d'assainissement, *Rapport général* (Nice: Imprimerie Administrative, 1893), p. 12.

9. Délibérations, 6 February 1905.

10. *Le Phare du littoral,* 1 April 1874, p. 2; 3 November 1874, p. 2; 22 January 1875, p. 2.

11. Ibid., 23 October 1877, p. 2.

12. Délibérations, 19 May 1875.

13. Ibid.

14. Ville de Nice, *Rapport à monsieur le maire sur la réforme des vidanges à Nice* (Nice: Imprimerie Administrative, 1876), pp. 12–23.

15. Latouche, *Histoire de Nice,* 2:73; Georges Haussmann, *Mémoires du Baron Haussmann,* vol. 3, *Grands travaux de Paris* (Paris: Victor-Havard, 1893), p. 116.

16. For detailed descriptions of Nice's climate, see Blanchard, *Le Comté de Nice,* pp. 76–83; Burnet, *Villégiature et tourisme,* pp. 70–80.

17. Ville de Nice, *Rapport . . . sur la réforme des vidanges,* p. 5.

18. See chapter 4 for a discussion of the impact of the 1882 crash.

19. *L'Eclaireur de Nice,* 21 October 1892, p. 1.

20. Unlike nontourist cities where governments often assumed a caretaker role during the hottest months, Nice usually reserved its ticklish political questions for the summer. This was particularly true of questions relating to sanitary reform. As the *Eclaireur de Nice* candidly pointed out in a series of articles discussing the city's sewers, "At the beginning of the winter season, at the moment when the tourists, fleeing the cold countries of the North, prepare to come and warm themselves on our coast, we think that it is our duty to suspend a debate which could well terrify our future guests" (26 October 1892, p. 1).

21. Délibérations, 24 May 1884.

22. [E. Durand-Claye], *Alfred Durand-Claye: 1841–1888* ([Paris]: Imprimerie de F. Leve [1889]), pp. 113–20.

23. Ville de Nice, *Assainissement de la ville de Nice,* pp. 3–4.

24. Ibid., pp. 7–9.

25. The administration must have known that Durand-Claye would recommend this solution because he had become known in Paris as "M. Tout-à-l'égout" (Mr. Everything-in-the-sewer); see Durand-Claye, *Alfred Durand-Claye,* p. 29.

26. Délibérations, 25 February 1885.

27. Ibid., 17 March 1887; Balestre computed the death rate from typhoid as 112 per 100,000 in 1886, a dismal figure that ranked Nice seventy-second out of seventy-eight major European cities.

28. In general, the principle of keeping sanitary sewers completely separate from storm drains prevails in the United States; some European cities, most notably in France, however, continue to rely on *tout-à-l'égout.*

29. *L'Eclaireur de Nice,* 21 October 1892, p. 1.

30. Ibid., 22 October 1892, p. 1.

31. Ibid., 21 October 1892, p. 1.

32. Compagnie Nationale de Travaux d'Utilité Publique et d'Assainissement, *Ville de Nice: Assainissement: Mémoire présenté à la séance de la Commission d'assainissement du 8 juillet 1893* (Paris: Imprimerie Charles Schlaeber, 1893), pp. 16–17.

33. *L'Eclaireur de Nice,* 21 October 1892, p. 1; Délibérations, 25 February 1892; Budget de la Ville de Nice, 1890.

34. *L'Eclaireur de Nice,* 27 August 1892, p. 3; 11 October 1892, p. 1.

35. Such attacks on Nice and especially on its sanitary system were a standard feature of each season. The Niçois, of course, thought that these attacks in the foreign press were provoked by payoffs from rival resorts hoping to profit by damaging Nice's reputation. An example of this kind of yellow journalism was provided in 1890 by *L'Etoile Belge* of Brussels which published a report from a reader living in Livorno, Italy, a city some sixteen hours by rail from Nice. The correspondent claimed that Nice was raging with typhoid fever, that Nice's hospital was full, and that two emergency hospitals had had to be built to deal with all the typhoid cases resulting from the city's contaminated water supply. The *Eclaireur,* probably with much justice, complained that this totally false report had been planted by rival resorts that had paid to have it published; see *L'Eclaireur de Nice,* 21 December 1890, p. 1.

36. Ibid., 3 July 1893, p. 2.

37. Ville de Nice, Commission consultative d'assainissement, *Rapport Général,* pp. 1–19; *L'Eclaireur de Nice,* 30 June 1893, p. 2; 2 July 1893, p. 2; 3 July 1893, p. 2.

38. *L'Eclaireur de Nice,* 3 July 1893, p. 2.

39. Ibid., 16 May 1893, p. 2; 24 October 1892, p. 1; Robert de Souza, *Nice: Capitale d'hiver* (Paris: Berger-Levrault, 1913), p. 208.

CONCLUSION

1. Mme. Caillaux had pumped six shots into the stomach of Gaston Calmette, the editor of *Le Figaro,* who was leading a press campaign to destroy her husband. She claimed that the gun had gone off by itself, and the jury believed her. See Shirer, *Collapse of the Third Republic,* pp. 115–16.

2. Ralph Schor, *Nice pendant la guerre de 1914–18* (Aix-en-Provence: La Pensée Universitaire), pp. 103–6.

3. For a discussion of postwar tourism, see Robert S. Rudney, "From Luxury to Popular Tourism: The Transformation of the Resort City of Nice" (Ph.D. diss., University of Michigan, 1979).

Sources

A BASIC PROBLEM CONFRONTING ALL HISTORIANS studying urban populations is the difficulty involved in quantitatively comparing the population of one socially or culturally defined geographical area to another. Despite the large amount of census data available for nineteenth-century France, necessary quantitative data are seldom available in a form suitable for this kind of inquiry: in almost all cases, basic population data exist only in a format designed to meet the needs of the organizations or agencies that commissioned the original data collection. Although this makes it a fairly straightforward matter to compare officially defined units, such as *départements,* to one another, it makes it difficult for a researcher to make geographical comparisons between areas that are physically, culturally, or socially identifiable, but which lie within a larger administrative unit. This is certainly the case with nineteenth-century French population data.

Census information of various kinds is readily available on the level of the *département.* (It is even possible to obtain French population data for the years 1851–1891 in machine-readable form. The information has been collected by the Inter-University Consortium for Political Research from the *Statistique générale de la France* and is mostly on the *département* level.) And occasionally census information is available for other sub-*département* units—*arrondissement, commune,* or *chef-lieu.* No compilations exist, however, for other units that are culturally homogeneous but lack official definition.

The main problem for an historian interested in examining the population of geographical units that lack official definition is one of aggregation. The fundamental sources exist. Anyone with sufficient zeal can consult the *Listes Nominatives,* which in essence are listings of individuals encountered in the census-taking process. The *Listes Nominatives* theoretically exist both in the appropriate Archives Départementales and in the various Archives Communales; it is usually best, however, to use them in one of the Archives Départementales as the communal archives are often badly managed, and many copies of the *Listes* have been destroyed. Using these sources is very tedious because of their very lack of aggregation. Although the information they contain, such as age, geographical origin, occupation, and the like is generally complete, they are simply lists of individuals and contain very little aggregated information. Thus, if demographic or ecological studies focusing on areas of France that are culturally distinct, but not officially defined, is to proceed on a quantitative level, methods must be found that will allow the creation of new levels of aggregation based on nominative data available in the *Listes Nominatives*. Ideally, such methods should provide the historian with complete control over both the definition of geographical units and the level of aggregation.

Although this kind of control was practically unattainable in the past because of the difficulty in collecting, organizing, and analyzing population information, the recent development of powerful and versatile electronic computing machinery has opened new vistas to population geographers and historians working in historical demography or human ecology. It is now possible for an historian equipped with an understanding of the procedures and techniques involved to have a degree of control over his data undreamed of only a few years ago. In analyzing the population structure of Nice, electronic data processing techniques have been combined with the analytical tools of both the urban historian and the population geographer to produce a more detailed understanding than had hitherto been possible.

The basic information upon which this section rests is a 10 percent random sample of records describing individual heads-of-households in Nice drawn from the *Listes Nominatives* in the Archives Municipales de Nice for the years 1872, 1891, and 1911. Besides the usual information concerning age, birthplace, occupation, marital status, and family situation, each record was coded to include the street address of each person, an essential component of any effort to study the geographical distribution of an urban population.

The availability of precise addresses allowed the use of a methodological device called the artificial block system, which is designed to give the researcher great flexibility in defining geographical space. Essentially, the artificial block system involves laying a grid pattern over an ordinary map. Each address can then be plotted according to its appropriate block and assigned a set of numerical coordinates that define its position in respect to every other cell in the grid. The size of the blocks is, of course, completely variable, and each researcher can choose whatever size seems most appropriate to him. After the blocking procedure is completed, it is relatively simple to combine groups of blocks to create reasonable approximations of actual physical or cultural neighborhoods. Although some imprecision results from the fact that neighborhoods thus created can never follow natural boundaries, this is greatly outweighed by the advantages of having control over the definition of geographical space. Moreover, the researcher has completely disaggregate data with which to work, because the basic unit of analysis remains the individual located within his block. One can choose an approprite level of aggregation and produce whatever numerical or statistical information is desired for the exact neighborhood chosen. This method helps to diminish problems resulting from the natural heterogeneity of larger areas. After placing each individual within the proper block, computations can be made for an individual block, for various physical and cultural neighborhoods, and for the city as a whole.

The result of this process is a series of figures which, if appropriately organized and presented, are in themselves sufficient to give a reader an understanding of the organization of urban space. While the information imparted is useful, the text-and-figure approach sometimes gives the reader the feeling that something has been left out. After all, the study of urban history is people and their living space; and the excitement of understanding the complexities of how populations interact with their physical environment is sometimes diminished when the understanding must be extracted from pages of numbers. Although urban historians usually implicitly or explicitly deal with spatial information, maps or other aids for the display of such information are too often absent. Leo Schnore in his useful essay, "Problems in the Quantitative Study of Urban History" in *The Study of Urban History,* ed. H. J. Dyos [New York: St. Martin's Press, 1968]), specifically calls for more research focusing on both the temporal and spatial dimensions of urban populations.

As a step toward meeting the needs of scholars working with information that is essentially spatial, modern computergraphic equipment developed primarily for use in engineering, medical, and aerospace environments can be invaluable. Any spatial information that can be given coordinate values—ranging from the location of brain tumors to housing choices made by nineteenth-century Niçois—can be displayed and analyzed by this system. Typically, users have complete control over the size, scale, and coloration of images and in minutes can electronically create maps that would otherwise take days or weeks to complete. Thus, it is a perfect complement to the analytical method described above—the areas in which one is interested can be displayed visually and analyzed quantitatively at the same time, a feature which adds a new dimension to the study of population. This examination of Nice illustrates the analytical possibilities inherent in the combination of these two methods. A much more detailed examination of the ecological dimensions of Nice's population is now in progress.

ARCHIVAL SOURCES

ARCHIVES NATIONALES

Série F^{1c} Esprit Public, Elections, Conseils Généraux, Conseils d'Arrondissement
    III Alpes-Maritimes (ancien département)
        1 Elections, 1792–1808
        2 Elections et comptes rendus administratives, 1808–1813
        3 Correspondence et divers, 1793–1813
    III Alpes-Maritimes (nouveau département)

1 Elections; Comptes rendus administratives, 1864–1877

2 Correspondence et divers, 1860–1870

Série F² Administration Départementale

I 106³⁴ Etrangers; Questions relative à la législation de l'ancien régime, An V [1796]–1825

I 990 Grande voirie et police du roulage, 1806–1832, Ain à Bouches-du-Rhône

II Alpes-Maritimes 1, Voirie urbaine 1810

Série F⁵ Comptabilité Départementale

II Alpes-Maritimes

1–6⁴ Comptes de recettes et dépenses, An III [1794]–1904

7–9⁴ Budgets, An XIII [1804]–1904

11 Affaires diverses relatives aux budgets, 1861–1904

13 Correspondence Divers, 1860–1880

Série F⁶ Comptabilité Communale

II Alpes-Maritimes 4 Nice

Série F⁷ Police Générale

12209 Talons de passes délivrées par le consulat générale de France en Angleterre, 1851

12338 Etats numerique du mouvement des étrangers 1839–40 et 1846–47

12341–12342 Correspondence et documents relatifs au service des passeports, 1845–1848

12343 Etats des passeports délivrées pour l'étranger à Bordeaux, 1847, et à Marseille, 1846–50

12357 Sociétés et associations: autorizations et surveillance, 1870–1912, Allier-Côtes-du-Nord

12581–12584 Police des étrangers, 1886–1906

Série F⁸ Police Sanitaire

180 Alimentation en eau des villes et communes, 1882–1902, Aisne-Alpes-Maritimes

Série F¹⁰ Agriculture

4527 Objets Généraux (1882–1918)

4528 Le Paillon, 1884–1946

Série F¹¹ Subsistances

2684 Statistique agricole annuelle des céréals et autres farineux alimentaires, 1862, Ain à Côtes-du-Nord

Série F¹² Commerce et Industrie

4481 Situation industrielle, 1830–1888, Alpes-Maritimes

6172–6174 Statistique industrielle et commerciale, 1869–1900

Série F¹⁴ Travaux Publics

955 Comptabilité du service des ponts et chaussées et de la navigation. Alpes-Maritimes-Apennins

1684 Routes nationale et ponts, 1840–95, Alpes-Maritimes

8558 Réseau du P.L.M.: Statistique, 1855–1898

8829 Chemins de fer. Avant projets et projets. Réseau du Nord. Enquête: Calais-Méditerranée par Amiens et Dijon, 1869–1873

12392 Adductions d'eau et égouts: Avis du conseil des ponts et chaussées, Pourvois en conseil d'état, 1833–1914

Série F^{19} Cultes

10928–10929 Culte anglican. Documents généraux et série départementale, An X–1904

Série F^{20} Statistique

710 Tableaux du mouvement des passeports pour l'étranger (1846–51, 1852, 1858–1861)

ARCHIVES DEPARTEMENTALES DES ALPES-MARITIMES

Série M Police

3 Rapports du police, Etat des voyageurs notables arrivées ou sortis de France

9–10 Rapports du police, Etat des voyageurs arrivées à Nice

23 Rapports du police, Rapports d'affairs et d'événements divers, 1860–70

24–50 Rapports du police

51 Rapports du police, Evénements divers

M Principauté de Monaco 29, Relations administratives avec la Principauté, Société des bains de mer, Casino, 1856–1893

1-M-1-5 Législation Sociale

Etrangers 9 Colonie anglaise, 1861–1877

Etrangers 10 Surveillance des sujets allemands, 1871–75

3e République, du préfet et sous préfets sur la situation du département et des arrondissements, 1872–74

3e République 39, Rapports sur affairs et événements divers, 1871–75

3e République 40, Rapports sur affairs et événements divers, 1881–85

3e République 41, Rapports sur affairs et événements divers, 1891–1902

III-M-2 Situation des ouvriers

IV-M Syndicats professionelles 15, Nice hotellerie, 1878–1925

IV-M Syndicats professionelles 12, Nice alimentation, 1876–1925; Commerçants, 1891–1902

IV-M Syndicats professionelles 13, Bâtiment

IV-M Syndicats professionelles 14, Transport, habillement

Série N Dépôt de mendicité

Série S Travaux Publics

401 S-1 Statistique-rapports, 1863–1894

401 S-5 Marche des trains, Horaires

412 S Tramways et bus 1-3

412 S-1 Demandes divers et concessions (enquête, 1870–74)

412 S-2 Divers, 1874–98

412 S-3 Conventions et convenants, homologation des tariffs, 1901–13

445 S-1-8 Police de la circulation, 1880–1914

504 S-1 Canal du Sainte-Thècle, avant projet, 1862–68

461 S-2 Le Paillon, Etablissement d'une route pour la construction du square Masséna, 1867

461 S-3 Le Paillon, Consolidation du radier sous le Casino Municipale, 1884–94

21-S-40 (1) Améliorations et travaux, Nice

ARCHIVES MUNICIPALES DE LA VILLE DE NICE

Série 1.0.3. Travaux

102 Compagnie Générale des Eaux, Déviation de la Vésubie

111 Compagnie Générale des Eaux, Mélanges des eaux de la Vésubie et de Ste.-Thècle

116 Compagnie Générale des Eaux, Avant Projet, 1863–64

258 Travaux d'assainissement du Paillon

290 Avant projet d'assainissement de la ville

293 Travaux d'assainissement. Lavage des égouts, Arrossage des Rues

Miscellaneous Dossiers

13 (0) 302 Etablissement des bains de mer à Nice, 1869–1921

1 303 Paillon, Couverture, 1877–1879

1.I.11 Prostitution, Plaintes des commerçants du quartier Croix-de-Marbre, Rue Masséna

Délibérations du Conseil Municipal de la Ville de Nice, 1860–1914

NEWSPAPERS

Le Baigneur. Journal hebdomadaire des villes d'eaux. 1 May 1881–13 June 1885.

La Chronique des stations hivernales de la Méditerranée. Journal politique et littéraire. Gazette des théâtres, beaux-arts. 1 October 1876–18 April 1877.

La Chronique niçoise. Journal littéraire, artistique et commercial. 18 November 1866–18 April 1867.

La Colonie étrangère. Saison du littoral. Edition d'hiver du "Schweizer Fremdenblatt" à Interlaken. Journal politique, littéraire, mondain, artistique et touristique avec la liste des étrangers. 3 November 1881–16 April 1899.

Le Commercial de Nice: Organe des intérêts industriel et commerciaux de Nice et du département. 18 August 1872–22 September 1872.

L'Eclaireur du littoral: Journal républicain quotidien. (Later *L'Eclaireur de Nice.*) April 1887–August 1914.

Gazette de Nice et des Alpes-Maritimes. 1887.

Gazette des étrangers. 1892.

L'Hivernal: Organe libre parleur des étrangers. 13 January 1883–17 March 1883.
Le Journal du littoral: Agriculture, horticulture, commerce, industrie, finances, connaissances utiles, faits-divers. 14 November 1880–1 March 1881.
The Mediterranean: Gazette des étrangers. 19 October 1882–14 February 1885.
Le Phare du littoral. 23 October 1870–1 January 1888.

BOOKS AND ARTICLES

A . . . de L . . . [Auguste de Louvais]. *Nice et ses environs, ou vingt vues dessinées d'après nature en 1812 dans les Alpes Maritimes.* Paris: Remoissenet, 1814.
Ackerknecht, Erwin H. "Anticontagionism between 1812 and 1867," *Bulletin of the History of Medicine* 22 (1948):562–93.
Ad. de R. *Nice et ses environs.* Paris: Lanée [1891].
Adenis, Jules. *Les Etapes d'un touriste en France: de Marseille à Menton.* Paris: A. Hennuyer, 1892.
Alpes-Maritimes, principauté de Monaco: Dictionnaire, annuaire et album. Paris: Ernest Flammarion [1903].
Ambayrac, M. *Nice et ses environs: Etude pittoresque et géologique.* Nice: Imprimerie Gauthier, 1882.
Améliorations à introduire dans le système d'égouts de Nice, rapport de l'ingenieur en chef des Alpes-Maritimes. Nice: Imprimerie Niçoise, 1884.
Les Anglais dans le Comté de Nice et en Provence depuis le XVIIIᵉ siècle. Nice: Editions des amis du Musée Masséna, 1934.
"Les Anglais sur la Riviera au Musée Masséna de Nice," édition spéciale de *Riviera Magazine,* February–March 1934.
Antier, Jean-Jacques. *Le Comté de Nice.* Paris: Editions France-Empire, 1970.
Ardouin-Dumazet, Victor-Eugène. *Voyage en France.* Vol. 13, *La Provence maritime, Marseille—Le Littoral—Iles d'Hyères—Maures—Estéral—Nice.* Paris: Berger-Levrault, 1898.
Arène. *Nice autrefois: "Souvenirs de cinquante ans."* Nice: Imprimerie du Commerce, 1910.
Armengaud, A. "Quelques aspects de l'hygiène publique à Toulouse au début du XXᵉ siècle." *Annales de démographie historique,* 1975, pp. 131–38.
Babeau, Albert. *Le Village sous l'ancien régime.* Paris: Perrin, 1915.
———. *La Ville sous l'ancien régime.* 2 vols. Paris: Didier, 1884.
Balestre, A. *Assainissement de Nice: Rapport au conseil municipal.* Nice: A. Gilleta, 1887.
Balestre, P.-L., and Grinda, Edouard. *Les Progrès de l'hygiène urbaine à Nice: Leur influence sur la santé publique.* XVᵢᵉᵐᵉ Congrès National de la Pro-

priété batie, Nice, 3–11 April 1911. Nice: Imprimerie Léo Barma, 1911.

Baratier, Edouard; Duby, Georges; and Hildesheimer, Ernest. *Atlas historique: Provence, Comtat Venaissin, Principauté de Monaco, Principauté d'Orange, Comté de Nice.* Paris: A. Colin, 1969.

Barety, A. "Le Voyage de Nice d'autrefois: d'Antibes à Gênes par la route." *Nice Historique* 15 (1913):169–85.

Barrier, Michèle. *L'Etude du tourisme: Problèmes de méthode et de répresentation cartographique dans l'est de la France.* Caen: Association des Publications de la Faculté des Lettres et Sciences Humaines de l'Université de Caen, 1964.

de Bartolomeis, Luigi. *Notizie topografiche e statistiche sugli stati sardi.* Book 2, Vol. 4. Torino: Tipografia Chirro e Mina, 1847.

Bazancourt, le Baron de. *Nice et ses souvenirs.* 2d ed. Nice: Imprimerie Société Typographique, 1861.

Beaumont, Albani. *Voyage historique et pittoresque du Comté de Nice.* Genève: Isac Bardin, 1787.

Bianchi, Blanche. *La Saison d'hiver à Cannes de 1870 à 1914.* Cannes: Equipe des historiens de Cannes, 1964.

Blanchard, Raoul. *Le Comté de Nice: Etude géographique.* Paris: Librairie Arthème Fayard, 1960.

Block, Maurice. *Dictionnaire de l'administration française.* Revised by Edouard Maguéro. Vols. 1–2. Paris: Berger-Levrault, 1905.

Blondel, M. F. *Rapport sur l'épidémie cholérique 1853–54 dans les établissements dépendant de l'administration général de l'assistance publique de la ville de Paris.* Paris: Imprimerie de P. Dupont, 1855.

Boniface, Léonce, and Hildesheimer, Ernest. "La Condition ouvrière à Nice en 1848." *Nice Historique* 42 (1959):22–30.

Bonnafont, J.-P. *Le Choléra devant l'Académie de Médecine: La Contagiosité et les quarantines.* Paris: Librairie J.-B. Baillière, 1885.

Borea, G. "Notes d'un hivernant à Nice avant l'annexion." *Nice Historique* 37 (1939):81–91.

———. "La Promenade des Anglais." *Nice Historique* 27 (1929):149–52.

Borel, Pierre. *Côte d'Azur.* Translated by Alan Ramsay. London: Nicholas Kaye, 1957.

Bouvier, Jean. *Le Krach de l'Union Générale (1878–1885).* Paris: Presses Universitaires de France, 1960.

———. "Sur les dimensions mesurables du fait financier: XIX et XX siècles." *Revue d'histoire économique et sociale* 46 (1968):161–84.

Boyer, Marc. "Hyères, station d'hivernants au XIXᵉ siècle." *Provence Historique* 12 (1962):139–65.

———. *Le Tourisme.* Paris: Editions du Seuil, 1972.

———. "Le Tourisme dans le sud-est méditerranéen français." *Bulletin de la Section de Géographie,* Ministère de l'éducation nationale, Comité des travaux historiques et scientifiques (1958), pp. 13–40. Paris: Imprimerie Nationale, 1959.

Braudel, Fernand. *The Mediterranean and the Mediterranean World in the Age of Philip II.* Vol. 1. Translated by Siân Reynolds. New York: Harper & Row, 1972.

de Brosses, Charles. *Lettres historiques et critiques sur l'Italie.* 3 vols. Paris: Ponthieu, An VII [1798].

Brun, F. A. *Promenades d'un curieux dans Nice.* Nice: Imprimerie et Lithographie Malvano-Mignon, 1894.

Burnel, A. *Etude sur Nice.* Nice: Imprimerie Société Typographique, 1856.

——. *Etude sur Nice.* 3d ed. Nice: Imprimerie Caisson, 1862.

Burnet, Louis. *Villégiature et tourisme sur les côtes de France.* Paris: "Bibliothèque des guides bleus," Librairie Hachette, 1963.

Cameron, Rondo. *France and the Development of Europe, 1800–1914: Conquests of Peace and Seeds of War.* Princeton: Princeton University Press, 1961.

Candy, M. *Rapport sur le choléra-morbus de Paris (épidémie de 1849) présenté à M. le maire et au conseil municipal de Lyon au nom d'une commission médicale* (Lyons: Imprimerie de Radenet, 1849.

Canestrier, Paul. *Nice terre de France: Essai historique.* Rodez: Imprimerie P. Carrere, 1940.

Caron, François. *An Economic History of Modern France.* Translated by Barbara Bray. New York: Columbia University Press, 1979.

Chadwick, Edwin. *Report on the Sanitary Condition of the Labouring Population of Great Britain.* London: H.M.S.O. 1842. Edited and Introduced by M. W. Flinn. Edinburgh: Edinburgh University Press, 1965.

Charmes, Gabriel. *Les Stations d'hiver et la Méditerranée.* Paris: Calmann Levy, 1885.

Clapham, J. H. *The Economic Development of France and Germany, 1815–1914.* 2d ed. Cambridge: Cambridge University Press, 1923.

Clough, Shepard B., and Cole, Charles W. *Economic History of Europe.* Rev. ed. Boston: D. C. Heath, 1946.

Compagnie Générale des Eaux de France. *Traités avec la ville de Nice pour la distribution des eaux de Sainte-Thècle.* Nice: Imprimerie spéciale du "Petit Niçois," 1895.

Compagnie Nationale de Travaux d'Utilité Publique et d'Assainissement. *Ville de Nice: Assainissement. Mémoire présenté à la séance de la Commission d'assainissement du 8 juillet 1893.* Paris: Imprimerie Charles Schlaeber, 1893.

Compan, André. *Histoire de Nice et de son comté.* Toulon: L'Astrado, 1973.

——. "La Société Niçoise en 1860." *Nice Historique* (Numéro spéciale du centennaire) 63 (1960):55–72.

Daumard, Adeline. "Une Source d'histoire sociale: L'Enregistrement de Paris en 1820 et 1847." *Revue d'histoire économique et sociale* 35 (1957):52–78.

Decaux, Alain. *Les Heures brillantes de la Côte d'Azur.* Paris: Librairie Académique Perrin, 1964.

Delgado, Alan. *The Annual Outing and Other Excursions.* London: George Allen & Unwin, 1977.

Demougeot, A. "Les Anglais à Nice pendant la paix d'Amiens, 1802–1803." *Recherches régionales (Côtes d'Azur et contrées limitrophes)* 3, no. 1 (1963):24–35.

———. "Présentation et texte d'un mémoire sur le commerce de Nice (1747–1749)," *Recherches régionales (Côte d'Azur et contrées limitrophes)* 9, no. 2 (1969):15–31.

Département des Alpes-Maritimes. *Rapport de l'ingénieur en chef, conseil général des Alpes-Maritimes, session de* . . . [1861–1872]. Nice: Imprimerie Canis, 1861–63; Typographie de V.-Eugène Gauthier, 1864–67; Typographie, Lithographie et Librairie Ch. Cauvin, 1868–72.

Département des Alpes-Maritimes. *Rapport du préfet et annexes, conseil général des Alpes-Maritimes, session de* . . . [1861–1872]. Nice: Imprimerie Canis, 1861–63; Typographie de V.-Eugène Gauthier, 1864–1867; Typographie, Lithographie et Librairie Ch. Cauvin, 1868–72.

Désert, Gabriel. "L'Enregistrement: Source d'histoire sociale." In *Actes du quatre-vingt-dixième congrès national des sociétés savantes, Nice, 1965: Section d'histoire moderne et contemporaine,* 1:33–53. 3 vols. Paris: Bibliothèque Nationale, 1966.

Devun, Jean. "L'Evolution de Nice: 1860 à 1960." *Recherches régionales (Côtes d'Azur et contrées limitrophes)* 10, no. 4 (1970):5–41.

———. "L'Evolution de Nice: 1860–1960, 2° partie." *Recherches régionales (Côtes d'Azur et contrées limitrophes)* 11, no. 1 (1971):1–63.

———. "L'Evolution de Nice: 1860–1960, 2° partie con't." *Recherches régionales (Côtes d'Azur et contrées limitrophes)* 11, no. 3 (1971):1–33.

Dorn, Harold F. "Mortality." *The Study of Population: An Inventory and Appraisal.* Edited by Philip M. Hauser and Otis Dudley Duncan. Chicago: University of Chicago Press, 1959.

Duchet, René. *Le Tourisme à travers les ages: Sa Place dans la vie moderne.* Paris: Vigot Frères, 1949.

Duffy, John. *A History of Public Health in New York City, 1625–1866.* New York: Russell Sage Foundation, 1968.

[Durand-Claye, E.] *Alfred Durand-Claye: 1841–1888* [Paris]: Imprimerie de F. Leve [1889].

Durandy, J. *Notes sur le plan régulateur des quartiers de St. Philippe et la Buffa.* Nice: Imprimerie et Lithographie Niçoise, 1880.

Durandy, M. *Rapport de la commission des travaux sur les mesures à adopter pour l'assainissement du Paillon, des égouts, et pour la vidange des fosses présenté dans la séance du 19 mai 1875.* Nice: Imprimerie Administrative, 1875.

Dyos, H. J. *Victorian Suburb: A Study of the Growth of Camberwell.* Leicester: Leicester University Press, 1961.

———, and Aldercroft, D. H. *British Transport: An Economic Survey from the Seventeenth Century to the Twentieth.* Leicester: Leicester University Press, 1969.

Faucher, Daniel, ed. *La France: Géographie-tourisme.* 6 vols. Paris: Librairie Larousse, 1951.

Féliciangeli, Daniel. "La Développement de Nice au cours de la second moitié du XVIII° siècle: Les Anglais à Nice," *Annales de la faculté des lettres et sciences humaines de Nice* 19 (1973):45–67.

Fenart, J. "Etude économique de l'agriculture dans les Alpes-Maritimes." *Recherches régionales (Côtes d'Azur et contrées limitrophes)* 4, no. 1 (1964): 1–8.

Fodéré, François-Emmanuel. *Voyage aux Alpes-Maritimes ou histoire naturelle, agraire, civile et médicale du Comté de Nice et pays limitrophes.* 2 vols. Paris: F. G. Levrault, 1821.

Fourastié, Jean, and Fourastié, Françoise. *Voyage et voyageurs d'autrefois.* Paris: Denoël, 1972.

Gallo, Max. "Pour une étude de la santé publique à Nice sous l'administration Sarde: Enquête sur le choléra à Nice en 1835." *Recherches régionales (Côtes d'Azur et contrées limitrophes)* 5, no. 3 (1965):41–53.

Ginier, Jean. *Géographie touristique de la France.* 2d ed. Paris: Société d'edition d'Enseignement Supérieur, 1974.

Girard, Prosper. *Les Eaux du Var et de la Vésubie. 1° Question de vie ou de mort pour la ville de Nice.* Nice: Imprimerie Anglo-Française, 1876.

———. *Les Eaux du Var et de la Vésubie. 3° Parallèle des projets du Var et de la Vésubie.* Nice: Imprimerie Anglo-Française, 1877.

Gonnet, Paul. "Archives fiscales et histoire social." *Revue d'histoire économique et sociale* 36 (1958):432–43.

———. "Archives fiscales et histoire urbaine." *Revue d'histoire économique et sociale* 35 (1957):41–51.

Grinda, Edouard. *La Question des eaux à Nice: Projet d'alimentation de la ville en eau potable par les sources du Vegay et de la Gravière, completées par les eaux de Ste.-Thècle et de la Vésubie. Discours prononcé à la séance du conseil municipal du 27 mars 1912.* Nice: Imprimerie de l'Eclaireur, 1912.

Guide des étrangers à Nice 1858–59 publié par l'office central des étrangers. Nice: Imprimerie Canis, 1858.

Guillaume, Pierre. *La Population de Bordeaux au XIX° siècle: Essai d'histoire sociale.* Paris: Armand Colin, 1972.

Haug, C. James. "Manuscript Census Materials in France: The Use and Availability of the *Listes Nominatives,*" *French Historical Studies* 12 (1979): 258–74.

———. "The Population Dynamics of a Tourist City: Nice, 1872–1911," *Proceedings of the Third Annual Meeting of the Western Society for French History,* pp. 421–27. Edited by Brison D. Gooch. College Station, Tex.: The Western Society for French History, 1976.

SOURCES

Haussmann, Georges. *Mémoires du Baron Haussmann.* Vol. 3, *Grandes travaux de Paris.* Paris: Victor-Havard, 1893.

Hemardinquier, Jean-Jacques. "Nice à l'heure du despotisme éclairé: Lettres et mémoires inedits de l'abbé Expilly." In *Actes du quatre-vingt-dixième congrés national des sociétés savantes. Nice, 1965: Section d'histoire moderne et contemporaine,* 1:249–76. Paris: Bibliothèque Nationale, 1966.

Henrey, Mrs. Robert. *Milou's Daughter Madeleine: A Sentimental Journey to the South of France.* New York: E. P. Dutton, 1955.

Hibbert, Christopher. *The Grand Tour.* London: Weidenfeld and Nicolson, 1969.

Hildesheimer, Ernest. "Le Développement de Nice depuis deux-cent-cinquante ans." *Le Charactère saisonnier du phénomène touristique: Ses conséquences économiques,* pp. 53–63. Aix-en-Provence: La Pensée Universitaire, 1963.

———. "Nice au milieu du XVIIIᵉ siècle: Rapport de l'intendant général Joanini." *Nice Historique* 71 (1968): 33–51, 80–95, 126–32.

Holt, Edgar. *The Making of Italy, 1815–1870.* New York: Atheneum, 1971.

Howarth, Patrick. *When the Riviera Was Ours.* London: Routledge & Kegan Paul, 1977.

Imbert, Gaston. *Esquisse de l'activité économique des Alpes-Maritimes.* Nice: Chambre de Commerce de Nice et des Alpes-Maritimes [1959].

———. "La Situation économique du département des Alpes-Maritimes lors de sa constitution en 1860." *Nice Historique* 64 (1961):68–80.

Imbert, Léo. "Le Voyage à Nice il y a cent ans de Chalons-sur-Saône à Nice: Note d'un hiverant." *Provence Historique* 3 (1953):131–40.

de Kick, Paul [Paul de Choulot]. *Souvenirs et impressions d'un sous-lieutenant ou Nice, ses environs et la Rivière de Gênes.* Paris: Imprimerie P. A. Desrosiers, 1842.

Lacoste, Alexandre. *Nice, pittoresque et practique.* Nice: Imprimerie S.-C. Cauvin, 1876.

Lairolle, Ernest. *Etude sur la contribution mobilière à propos de son augmentation progressive à Nice.* Nice: Imprimerie Victor-Eugène Gauthier, 1888.

Lampard, Eric E. "Urbanization and Social Change," *The Historian and the City.* Cambridge: Cambridge University Press, 1963.

Latouche, Robert. *Histoire de Nice.* Vol. 1, *Des Origines à 1860.* Vol. 2, *De 1860 à 1914.* Vol. 3, *Epoque contemporaine.* Nice: Ville de Nice, 1951–65.

———. *Histoire du Comté de Nice.* Paris: Bovin, 1932.

———. "La Situation économique et politique du Comté de Nice pendant les premières années de la Restauration Sarde (1814–1823)." *Nice Historique* 24 (1926):42–47.

Lefèvre, A. and L. *Projet de distribution des eaux dans la ville de Nice.* Nice: Imprimerie Canis Frères, 1858.

Legrand, Patrick, and Legrand, Odile. "La rue d'Antibes et le quartier de la croisette à Cannes." *Annales de la faculté des lettres et sciences humaines de Nice* (1976), pp. 157–91.

160

Leonard, Charlene. *Lyon Transformed: Public Works of the Second Empire, 1853–1864.* University of California Publications in History, no. 57. Berkeley: University of California Press, 1961.

Lèques, Paulette. "Tourism hivernal et vie mondaine à Nice de 1860 à 1881: Cercles et salons." *Annales de la faculté des lettres et sciences humaines de Nice* (1973), pp. 93–101.

Lescure, Jean. *Crises générales et périodiques de surproduction.* 2d ed. Paris: J.-B. Sirey, 1910.

Liautaud, Colette. "Les Baumettes, campagne, faubourg puis quartier de Nice." *Recherches régionales (Côtes d'Azur et contrées limitrophes)* 10, no. 3 (1970):3–38.

MacCannell, Dean. *The Tourist: A New Theory of the Leisure Class.* New York: Schocken, 1976.

Mariotti, Giuliana. *Storia del turismo.* Roma: Edizioni Saturnia, 1958.

Martini, Josette. "L'Avenue de la gare à Nice." *Recherches Régionales (Côtes d'Azur et contrées limitrophes)* 3, no. 3 (1963):14.

Médecin, Jean, et al. *Livre du centenaire du rattachement de Nice à France.* Nice: Imprimerie Meyerbeer, 1960.

Melandri, Hellé. "Les Anglais à Nice au XVIIᵉ et XVIIIᵉ siècle." *Nice Historique* 57 (1954):41–50.

Meller, H. E. *Leisure and the Changing City, 1870–1914.* London: Routledge & Kegan Paul, 1976.

Le Mémorial de Nice, 1960. Nice: Editions de l'Armanac Nissart, 1961.

Mérimée, Prosper. *Lettres à Viollet-le-duc (documents inedits, 1839–1870).* Vol. 1 of *Oeuvres complètes de Prosper Mérimée.* Paris: Librairie Ancienne Honoré Champion, 1927.

Merquiol, André. *La Côte d'Azur dans la littérature française.* Nice: Editions Jacques Dervyl, 1949.

Millin, A. L. *Voyage en Savoie, en Piémont, à Nice et à Gênes.* 2 vols. Paris: C. Wasserman, 1816.

Mitchell, B. R. *European Historical Statistics, 1750–1970.* New York: Columbia University Press, 1976.

Nice-Express: Guide pratique de la ville de Nice et de ses environs. Nice: Imprimerie Niçoise [1886].

Nice Indicateur: Guide de l'étranger à Nice. Nice: Imprimerie Niçoise, 1893.

Notice sur l'état de la question des eaux en août 1901. Nice: Imprimerie Langoise [1901].

Papon, S. *Voyage dans le département des Alpes-Maritimes. avec la description de la ville et du terroir de Nice, de Menton, de Monaco, etc.* Paris: Imprimerie de Crapelet, 1804.

Peters, Michael. *International Tourism: The Economics and Development of the International Tourist Trade.* London: Hutchinson, 1969.

Pietri, A. "Nice capital touristique." *Actes du quatre-vingt-troisième Congrès National des Sociétés Savantes, Aix-Marseille, 1958, Bulletin de la section de géographie,* pp. 209–43. Paris: Imprimerie Nationale, 1959.

————. "Le Paillon, Torrent de Nice: Essai d'étude d'un cours d'eau des préalpes Méditerranéennes." Abrégé de la thèse soutenue devant la faculté des lettres et des sciences humaines d'Aix-Marseille, le 30 avril 1955.

Pimlott, J. A. R. *The Englishman's Holiday: A Social History.* 1947; reprint ed., Hassocks, Sussex: Harvester Press, 1976.

Planchet, Edmond. "Monte Carlo." *Revue des deux mondes* 55 (15 January 1883):433–54.

Rambert, Gaston. *Marseille, la formation d'une grande cité moderne: Etude de géographie urbaine.* Marseilles: Imprimerie du *Sémaphore,* 1934.

Robinson, H. *"Aspect" Geographics: A Geography of Tourism.* London: McDonald and Evans, 1976.

Rosen, George. *A History of Public Health.* New York: MD Publications, 1958.

Rosenberg, Charles E. *The Cholera Years: The United States in 1832, 1849, and 1866.* Chicago: University of Chicago Press, 1962.

Roubaudi, Louis. *Nice et ses environs.* Paris: Allonard, 1843.

Roux, Joseph. *Statistique des Alpes-Maritimes.* 2 vols. Nice: Imprimerie et Librairie Ch. Chauvin, 1862.

Rudney, Robert S. "From Luxury to Popular Tourism: The Transformation of the Resort City of Nice." Ph.D. dissertation, University of Michigan, 1979.

Say, Léon. "La Politique financière de la France." *Journal des économistes* 20 (1882):157–76.

Schnore, Leo. "Problems in the Quantitative Study of Urban History." *The Study of Urban History.* Edited by H. J. Dyos. New York: St. Martin's Press, 1968.

Scoffier, Edouard, and Blanchi, Félix. *Le "Consiglio d'Ornato" 1832–1860.* Nice: Imprimerie Meyerbeer [1960].

Seguran, Victor-Emanuel. *Les Rues de Nice: Chroniques historiques et descriptives sur le vieux et le nouveau Nice.* Nice: Imprimerie V.-Eug. Gauthier, 1888.

Simon, John. *English Sanitary Institutions Reviewed in Their Course of Development, and in Some of Their Political and Social Relations.* 1890; reprint ed., New York: Johnson Reprint, 1970.

Smollett, Tobias. *Travels through France and Italy.* Vol. 5 of *Miscellaneous Works of Tobias Smollett,* 4th ed. Edinburgh: Sylvester Doig and Andrew Stirling, 1811.

Souza, Robert de. *Nice: Capitale d'hiver.* Paris: Berger-Levrault, 1913.

Sussman, George D. "Carriers of Cholera and Poison Rumors in France in 1832," *Societas—À Review of Social History* 3 (1973):232–51.

Thomas, A.-L. *Oeuvres complètes,* vol. 6. Paris: Verdière, 1825.

Tresse, René. "L'Etablissement de la voie ferrée dans l'arrondissement de Grasse, 1852–1882." *Revue d'histoire économique et sociale* 47 (1970): 353–72.

Ustrac, F. D', et al. *Nice-exposition.* Paris: Imprimerie A. Labure, 1884.

Vigier, Philippe. *Essai sur la répartition de la propriété foncière dans la région alpine, son évolution des origines du cadastre à la fin du second empire.* Paris: S.E.V.P.E.N., 1963.

Ville de Nice. *Assainissement de la Ville de Nice: Rapport de M. A. Durand-Claye.* Nice: Imprimerie Nouvelle, 1884.

Ville de Nice. *Cahier des charges de l'enterprise du service du balayage et de l'enlèvement des boues.* Nice: Imprimerie Administrative, 1875.

Ville de Nice, Service de la voirie urbaine. *Cahier des charges de l'enterprise du service du balayage et enlèvement des ordures et immondices et de l'enlèvement des boues et poussières.* Nice: Imprimerie Nouvelle, 1884.

Ville de Nice. *Question des eaux, alimentation des fontaines publiques et distribution d'eaux potables aux habitants.* Nice: Imprimerie Caisson, 1863.

Ville de Nice. *La Question des eaux, traités de 1864 à 1909.* 2 vols. Vol. 1. Nice: Imprimerie Niçoise, 1912. Vol. 2, Documents annexes. Nice: Imprimerie de *l'Eclaireur,* 1912.

Ville de Nice. *Rapport à monsieur le maire sur la réforme des vidanges à Nice.* Nice: Imprimerie Administrative, 1876.

Ville de Nice. Commission consultative d'assainissement. *Rapport général.* Nice: Imprimerie Administrative, 1893.

Warner, Sam B. *Streetcar Suburbs: The Process of Growth in Boston, 1870–1900.* New York: Atheneum, 1969.

Wylie, J. C. *The Wastes of Civilization.* London: Faber and Faber, 1959.

Young, Arthur. *Travels during the Years 1787, 1788, & 1789 Undertaken More Particularly with a View of Ascertaining the Cultivation, Wealth, Resources, and National Prosperity of the Kingdom of France.* 2d ed. 2 vols. 1794; reprint ed., New York: AMS Press, 1970.

Zeldin, Theodore. *France: 1848–1945.* Vol. 1, *Ambition, Love, and Politics.* Oxford: Clarendon Press, 1973.

Index

DATE DUE